40¢

JANUARY BIBLE STUDY 2014
Personal Study Guide

Colossians
Christ Is All
You Need

D1124863

LifeWay Press®
Nashville, TN

ISBN: 978-1-4158-7807-1
Item: 005558774

Subject Area: Bible Studies
Dewey Decimal Classification Number: 227.7
Subject Heading: BIBLE. N.T. COLOSSIANS—STUDY \ JESUS CHRIST \
CHRISTIAN LIFE
Printed in the United States of America

Adult Ministry Publishing
LifeWay Church Resources
One LifeWay Plaza
Nashville, TN 37234-0175

We believe the Bible has God for its author; salvation for its end; and truth,
without any mixture of error, for its matter and that all Scripture is totally
true and trustworthy. To review LifeWay's doctrinal guidelines, please visit
www.lifeway.com/doctrinalguideline.

Lesson Photos: Biblical Illustrator Photos

Contents

INTRODUCTION

Colossians: Christ Is All You Need

You cannot live the Christian life. If that statement sounds discouraging or inaccurate—I understand. It seems more loving to say, "You can do it. Just keep trying. God will bless your efforts." As a Baptist pastor, I've delivered my fair share of "try harder, do more, be stronger" messages.

For years, I lived and taught that spiritual growth was the result of consistently engaging in the spiritual disciplines. If I wanted a stronger relationship with God, I needed to pray more, study more, share more, serve more, give more, and go more. If I did those things consistently, then I would experience spiritual growth.

Unfortunately, the opposite happened. Instead of spiritual growth, I grew weary and overwhelmed. There was no way to keep up with the demands of life and religion. I gained biblical knowledge and personal discipline, but it didn't lead to life.

In time, God helped me see that growth in Christ is not trying harder, but trusting more. When I finally accepted that sheer determination is not the key to spiritual growth, the result has been a life of growth and freedom.

I've said a lot in a few paragraphs. Let me back up and share a story that will bring everything in perspective.

On the morning of August 27, 2004, I was trying to pray. I just couldn't do it. Instead of praying, my mind raced from one thing to the next. I had things to do, problems to solve, people to meet, goals to accomplish, and expectations to live up to. After several failed attempts to stay focused, I decided to write my thoughts in a journal. I wrote everything that I needed to do. I wrote down everything that people told me I had to be. I also wrote every goal I was trying to accomplish.

Over the next 45 minutes, I jotted down 15 personal concerns, 26 family concerns, and 89 work-related concerns. There were 130 identifiable issues that were pressing for my time and attention.

All of them seemed important. On a personal side, I wanted to be a great Christian. To be a great Christian, I was taught that I needed to be a soul-winner, servant, student of God's Word, giver, prayer-warrior, and disciple maker. I needed to be more holy, more gracious, more loving, more faithful, more patient, and more compassionate. I needed to memorize Scripture, put on my spiritual armor, ntercede for the sick, and walk in faith. That is just 16 of the 130 things on the list.

When I finished the list, it was the first time that the weight of expectations really hit me. Every time I focused on one area, something else seemed to go lacking. When I tried to pray more, I didn't share the gospel as often. When I tried to share the gospel more, I didn't memorize Scripture sufficiently. When I attempted to memorize more Scripture, I felt guilty for not serving more at church.

I constantly felt like I was letting God down. On the morning of August 27, I had a moment of unbelievable clarity. I cannot do it! There is no way I can fulfill every expectation. There's not enough time in the day to do everything that I feel needs to be done. I don't have enough discipline or inherent goodness to live up to God's perfect standards. I could not control or accomplish the 130 things spinning in my head at that moment.

No sooner did the thought come to mind than these words followed. "Come to Me, all of you who are weary and burdened, and I will give you rest. All of you, take up My yoke and learn from Me, because I am gentle and humble in heart, and you will find rest for yourselves. For My yoke is easy and My burden is light" (Matt. 11:28-30).

I can remember thinking, "Either Jesus is lying or I have greatly missed the Christian life." I knew Jesus would never lie, so the misunderstanding must be on my side. I prayed through my frustration. I said, "God, this isn't easy. The burden of the Christian life is not light. There are so many things to do, and be, and accomplish. How can this statement be true?"

In the silence of the moment, three little words stood out. "Come to Me." They were there all the time. In my hurry to do the right things, I missed an important step. Jesus' first words are an invitation to be with Him. In all my efforts to do something for God, I missed what Jesus was asking of me. He said, "Come to Me."

In the years that followed, God has taught me an incredible truth. Christianity is not about doing things *for* God; it is about being *with* God. When we are with God, in intimate fellowship, God lives His life through us.

Once this truth penetrated my heart, I started to see it elsewhere in Scripture. Jesus taught this principle when He spoke of the vine and the branches. "Remain in Me, and I in you.

Just as a branch is unable to produce fruit by itself unless it remains on the vine, so neither can you unless you remain in Me. I am the vine; you are the branches. The one who remains in Me and I in him produces much fruit, because you can do nothing without Me" (John 15:4-5). When we remain in Christ, He produces fruit through us. Our part is to remain in Him; His part is to live through us. This principle is also seen in the following passages. Words and phrases have been italicized for emphasis.

> He also appointed 12—He also named them apostles—*to be with Him,* to send them out to preach (Mark 3:14).

> and I no longer live, but *Christ lives in me.* The life I now live in the body, I live by faith in the Son of God, who loved me and gave Himself for me (Gal. 2:20).

> *Together with Christ Jesus* He also raised us up and seated us in the heavens (Eph. 2:6).

When I realized that my part was to be with Him, remain in Him, or abide in Him—I saw that His yoke was easy and His burden was light. I didn't have 130 things to do. I had one thing to do. My responsibility was to be with Christ and He would live His life through me.

You've heard part of my story. Now I have some questions for you. Do you feel overwhelmed by the demands of the Christian life? Do you ever feel like you're going through the motions of Christianity? Are you weary and worn down by the Christian routine? Are you so busy doing good things that you don't have time to rest, reflect, and refresh?

If so, heed the words of Christ: "Come to Me." The invitation of Christ is extended to all who are weary and burdened. He's not asking you to bring anything. He just wants you to come.

You may have a number of reservations about what I've shared. "What about the disciplines of the Christian faith? There is more to spiritual growth than just being with Christ. Someone has to do something. Someone has to give, and someone has to go, and someone has to work. We all can't just sit around."

The issue is not being versus doing; the issue is doing from the overflow of being.

I understand the concerns. I pushed back on these areas as well. Hopefully, this next statement will alleviate some tension. When we are with Christ, He will give us plenty to do. The issue is not being versus doing; the issue is doing from the overflow of being. Will we allow our actions to be the overflow of an intimate relationship with Jesus Christ?

Colossians: Christ is All You Need is a study to help you experience the abundant life in Christ. Jesus said that He came so that we might "have life and have it in abundance" (John 10:10). This study will help you move away from performance-based religion and step into the freedom of a relationship with Christ.

In order for that to happen, we must see ourselves from God's perspective and learn to rest in what we discover. As we work through Paul's letter to the church in Colossae, we will see that believers are rooted in Him, free in Him, built up in Him, hidden in Him, complete in Him, forgiven in Him, and seated with Him. We are secure in Christ because "the entire fullness of God's nature dwells bodily in Christ" (2:9). Our life is in Christ, and He lives through us.

In contrast to a human-centered approach to God, Paul argued that Christ is preeminent in everything and He alone is the source for the Christian life. In order to stress the fullness of the believer's life in Christ, Paul emphasized our position and possessions in Christ. At least 15 times in Colossians Paul used phrases like "in Christ," "in Him," "in God," or "in the Lord."

Paul's purpose in writing the Letter to the Colossians was to remind believers that Christ is all we need. It sounds simplistic, it sounds naïve, it may even sound cliché, but Christ is all we need.

If you are tired of performance-based religion, this study is for you. If you are overwhelmed by religious routines and if you are searching for the abundant life, I encourage you to take this journey with me through Colossians. If you have a sneaking suspicion that there's more to the Christian life than what you're tapping into, just keep reading. You are on the right track. The questions that linger are invitations to deeper intimacy with God.

May God free, empower, convict, and encourage you through the truths of Christ found in the Letter to the Colossians.

BITHYNIA AND PONTUS

GALATIA

MYSIA

ASIA

Caesarea (Mazaca)

CAPPADOCIA

Smyrna
Sardis
LYDIA
Ephesus
Hermus R.

Samos

Maeander R.

Laodicea
Colossae
PHRYGIA
PISIDIA

Antioch in Pisidia
Iconium

LYCAONIA

COMM

Miletus
CARIA

Lystra

Derbe

CILICIA

Patmos

Halicarnassus

Cos
Cnidus

LYCIA
Attalia
Perga
PAMPHYLIA

Taurus Mountains

Tarsus

Issus

Antioch

Alepp

Rhodes
Rhodes

Patara

Seleucia
Tracheotis

Seleucia
Pieria

Orontes R.

SYRI

Hamath

Crete

Salamis

Cyprus

Paphos

Tripolis

P
(Ta

Damascus

MEDITERRANEAN SEA

Tyre

Caesarea Maritima

Jordan R.

Philadelphia
(Amman)

Jerusalem

Gaza
JUDEA

*DEAD
SEA*

NABATEA

Alexandria

Pelusium

EGYPT

Memphis

Nile R.

0   50   100   150   200 Miles
0   50   100 150   200 Kilometers

CHAPTER 1

You Are Secure In Christ

COLOSSIANS 1:15-20

A young couple has been trying to have a baby for years, and the doctor just confirmed their greatest fear. They had another miscarriage. Grieving and in search of encouragement, they contact their pastor. He listens and sympathizes with their pain. The only words that come to mind are, "I'm sorry this happened. I'll pray for you. During this difficult time, try to remember that Christ is all you need."

Mike is driving home from the factory for the last time. After 21 years of faithful service, he just got laid off. Due to budget issues, middle management was the first to go. He's embarrassed. He's hurt. He has no idea of what to say to his wife. When he arrives at home, his wife greets him at the door with a kiss. He can't hold it in. In a moment of emotion and frustration, he tells her everything that happened. She tries to console him, but words don't seem like enough. Finally she says, "Mike, I love you and I'm proud of you. You didn't do anything wrong. We're going to be okay. Besides, Christ is all we need."

Sara has been a part of a recovery group for five months. As a teenager, she became addicted to meth. It almost destroyed her life. The group facilitator asks the participants, "Do you feel like you're better equipped to resist temptation?" One by one, recovering addicts affirm their newfound strength. "I've made it this far, I can do it." "Addiction is a battle of the mind and my mind is stronger." "It's been two years for me. I'm confident that I can stay clean." As Sara listens, she can't help but feel like an outsider. She doesn't feel stronger. In fact, it feels like the temptation is stronger than ever. She shares her assessment. The facilitator says, "I know you feel weak. Your mind tells you that you can't live without drugs. But keep your focus on Christ. He is all you need."

Christ is all you need.

We want to believe that statement. We want to know that when our hopes are dashed, and our lives are turned upside down, and when we are wrestling with sin, Christ is enough. Inside we may even believe it at some level. In light of eternity, Christ is all we need to get to heaven.

But our eternal destination is not our only concern. We need answers to temporal questions as well. Is Christ enough for a broken heart? Is He enough to calm our fears? Is He enough to provide food for our families, and give direction to our lives, and destroy the grip of sin? As Christians, we're grateful that Christ secures our eternal destination, but can He also meet our immediate needs?

LEARNING ACTIVITY

Not Enough

Many life experiences seem to communicate "not enough" to us. They seemingly mock our inability and insufficiency. Here are some examples:

Divorce: Your love is not enough.
Job termination: Your work/production is not enough.
Bankruptcy: Your balance/assets are not enough.
Illness: Your body is not enough.
Doubt/Confusion: Your wisdom is not enough.

What other life experiences communicate "not enough"?

As I stated in the introduction, the entire Letter to the Colossians can be summarized in one statement: Christ is all you need. However, to understand the depth of that statement, we need to understand the context of this letter. Let's spend a few moments diagnosing the condition and the setting of the church in Colossae.

The entire letter to the Colossians can be summarized in one statement: Christ is all you need.

A CLOSER LOOK

Colossians At a Glance

Who were the recipients of the letter?
A young church showing remarkable gospel progress and potential.

Where did they live?
Colossae was located in the Lycus River Valley of Asia Minor, 100 miles east of Ephesus and near the cities of Laodicea and Hierapolis. The population of Colossae was a mix of Gentiles and Jews.

Why did Paul write the letter?
Epaphras, a key leader in the church, paid Paul a visit in Rome (Paul was in prison there) and informed the apostle of certain heretical teachings that were bring spread in the Colossian church.

What were the particular threats Paul addressed?
(1) Greek philosophy, whose preconceived ideas about creation led to a rejection of both Christ's deity and humanity; (2) Jewish legalism, which asserted that Christ's death was not enough for either salvation or sanctification.

What is the major theme of Colossians?
Christ provides everything believers need for salvation and the Colossian heresy had nothing to add to what Jesus has already accomplished.

The church at Colossae was young and growing. They were grounded in the gospel (1:23), they were growing in the gospel (vv. 5-6), and they were living the gospel (vv. 4). Their maturity was demonstrated by their faith in Christ and their love for all the saints (v. 4). Paul's overall encouragement to the church was to continue on the path they started. "Therefore, as you have received Christ Jesus the Lord, walk in Him, rooted and built up in Him and established in the faith, just as you were taught, overflowing with gratitude" (2:6-7). The church had been given an incredible foundation.

While the church was moving in the right direction, it was not exempt from veering off course. They lived in a city that was drenched in pagan influences. The church was comprised of a mixture of Jews and Gentiles, both bringing remnants of their former lives into the church. Due to certain heretical teachings popping up in that region, the leadership was understandably cautious.

The primary leader mentioned in the Colossian church was Epaphras. While Paul never identified Epaphras as the one who started the church, he indicated that he was heavily involved with its formation. Epaphras was the one who taught them the gospel, and he was the one who reported their condition to Paul (1:7-8). Due to his concern over possible heresy, Epaphras made a 1,300-mile trip to Rome to visit Paul in prison. Colossians was Paul's reply to the concerns of Epaphras.

Based on the contents of the letter, it would seem that the church had not yet been infected with heresy. However, the danger of possible infection was real. From that perspective, Colossians was a preventative letter.

To fully grasp the teachings of Colossians, it is important to understand the heretical teachings that threatened the church. False religious teachers rarely teach something that completely rejects established truth. Instead, they add something to the truth or they twist the truth to fit their ideas. In this case, false teachers were attempting to infuse Christian doctrine with a mixture Greek philosophy and Jewish legalism. The result was a departure from Christ-centered living and a return to performance-based religion.

The first challenge came from Greek philosophy. When Greek philosophy was added to Christian doctrine, it attacked the nature and sufficiency of Christ. Let's begin by discussing the attack against Christ's nature.

There was a group in the first-century church that rejected the nature of Christ (both His deity and His humanity). Their background in Greek philosophy led them to believe that God was good and matter was evil. Therefore, God would never become a man, because that would make Him evil. Consequently, Jesus (the man) could not be God. Paul confronted this belief by stating, "For the entire fullness of God's nature dwells bodily in Christ" (2:9).

Not only did some people reject Christ's divinity, they also rejected His humanity. The incarnation of Christ (God becoming flesh) did not make logical sense. From their perspective, God could not have created evil matter. If matter is evil, then Jesus could not be human; rather, He was an emanation from God. To combat that teaching, Paul stressed that God did become a man in the Person of Jesus Christ. "For God was pleased to have all His fullness dwell in Him, and through Him to reconcile everything to Himself... He has reconciled you by His physical body through His death" (1:19-20,22). In addition to heretical teachings about Christ's nature, there were also people who believed that Christ was not sufficient for salvation. The Greeks loved knowledge and they took pride in the complexities of their philosophy. It was inconceivable to them that Christ was sufficient for salvation because the gospel was too simplistic (1 Cor. 1:22-23). Everyone could understand it. If everyone could understand it, then it must be lacking

Left: Tel Colossae near the modern town of Honaz, Turkey.

depth. This group claimed to receive special visions that led to deeper knowledge (Col. 2:18). They taught that salvation was the result of Christ plus knowledge. In order to challenge this false teaching, Paul reminded them that God's mystery is Christ Himself (2:2).

After addressing issues related to Greek philosophy, Paul turned his attention to concerns involving Jewish legalism. On the surface, Jewish legalism did not sound as harmful. The legalists never rejected the nature of Christ. That was a step in the right direction. However, the emphasis they placed on Jewish customs made them equally dangerous.

The moment anything is added to Christ for salvation,
it is a different gospel. The Greeks added knowledge to Christ;
the Jewish legalists added circumcision to Christ.

Jewish legalists taught that circumcision was necessary for salvation. In so doing, they fell into the same trap as those who embraced Greek philosophy. The moment anything is added to Christ for salvation, it is a different gospel. The Greeks added knowledge to Christ; the Jewish legalists added circumcision to Christ. Either way, they denied the sufficiency of Christ. Paul challenged this teaching by saying, "You were also circumcised in Him with a circumcision not done with hands, by putting off the body of flesh, in the circumcision of the Messiah" (2:11). He goes on to say, "In Christ there is not Greek and Jew, circumcision and uncircumcision ... but Christ is all and in all" (3:11). In other words, Christ is all you need.

Jewish legalists also considered self-denial to be the primary path to spiritual growth. From their perspective, a person grew spiritually by avoiding or depriving themselves of certain pleasures. In rebuttal, Paul asked, "If you died with the Messiah to the elemental forces of this world, why do you live as if you still belonged to the world? Why do you submit to regulations: 'Don't handle, don't taste, don't touch'? All these [regulations] refer to what is destroyed by being used up; they are commands and doctrines of men" (2:20-22). He went on to say, these teachings have "a reputation of wisdom by promoting ascetic practices, humility, and severe treatment of the body, they are not of any value in curbing self-indulgence" (v. 23).

Finally, the Jewish legalists emphasized keeping the Jewish dietary laws and observing holy days. Paul reminded the Colossians that ceremonialism does not make us right with God nor does it keep us right with God. "Therefore, don't let anyone judge you in regard to food and drink or in the matter of a festival or a new moon or a Sabbath day" (2:16). Those things were a shadow, but Christ is the substance (v. 17). Christ is all you need.

Christ is enough. He is enough to save you. He is enough to develop you. He is enough to sustain you. He is enough to keep you. Christ is all you need.

If the Colossian believers allowed Greek philosophy to influence their teachings, they would eventually reject the nature and sufficiency of Christ. If they allowed Jewish legalism to creep into their teachings, they would reject the sufficiency of Christ and add ceremonialism and self-denial to spiritual growth. With each challenge, Paul pointed back to the same answer: Christ is enough. He is enough to save you. He is enough to develop you. He is enough to sustain you. He is enough to keep you. Christ is all you need.

Left: The Mamertine prison in Rome, Italy, where Paul was imprisoned at one time. It is beneath the church of Giuseppe dei Falegname in modern Rome. The lower chamber was probably initially a cistern and dated as early as the 6th century B.C.

Match the Philosophy

Match the two challenges Paul addressed in Colossians to the appropriate description. Give contemporary application and examples of that to today's culture.

Challenge	Matching Description	Application and Examples
1. Greek philosophy	a. "I'm strong enough"	
2. Jewish legalism	b. "I'm smart enough"	

Answers 1.b; 2.a

Based on the specific teachings that threatened the Colossian church, the Letter to the Colossians is considered the most Christ-centered book in the Bible. The sufficiency and nature of Christ are emphasized throughout the book. Both are set up with Paul's description of Christ's nature in chapter one. Jesus is described as God (1:15), Creator (v. 16), Ruler (v. 17), Savior (v. 20), Sustainer (v. 17), and Head of the church (v. 18).

Based on who Christ is, our position is secure. Paul helps us see that we are rooted in Him, free in Him, built up in Him, hidden in Him, complete in Him, forgiven in Him, and seated with Him. We are secure in Christ because "the entire fullness of God's nature dwells bodily in Christ" (2:9). Our life is in Christ, and He lives through us.

As in many of Paul's letters, he started with doctrine and moved to application. Colossians is no different. Chapters 1–2 describe correct belief; chapters 3–4 encourage correct behavior.

Now that context has been established and the theme has been shared, let's turn our attention to the concept that believers are secure in Christ. Our security is connected to Christ's nature. Read through Paul's description of Christ's nature from Colossians 1:15-20. Pay close attention to references related to His nature.

> He is the image of the invisible God, the firstborn over all creation. For everything was created by Him, in heaven and on earth, the visible and the invisible, whether thrones or dominions or rulers or authorities—all things have been created through Him and for Him. He is before all things, and by Him all things hold together. He is also the head

of the body, the church; He is the beginning, the firstborn from the dead, so that He might come to have first place in everything. For God was pleased to have all His fullness dwell in Him, and through Him to reconcile everything to Himself by making peace through the blood of His cross—whether things on earth or in heaven.

There are at least six aspects of Christ's nature represented in these verses. Each aspect strengthens our sense of security by revealing the depth of Christ's character and ability. Let's take a few moments to describe each part of Christ's nature and show how it relates to the Christian life.

1. Jesus is God (Col. 1:15,19).

"He is the image of the invisible God ... For God was pleased to have all His fullness dwell in Him."

Jesus was not just a good man, a miracle worker, a great prophet, or a revolutionary leader. Jesus is God. He is the "image of the invisible God." If you want to know what God is like—look no further than Christ. If you want to see the wisdom of God, look to Christ. If you want to see the mercy of God, look to Christ. If you want to see the power of God, the grace of God, the truth of God, the glory of God, the heart of God, then look to Christ. All the fullness of God dwells in Him. Jesus is God.

WORD STUDY

"Image" (1:15)

The word translated as "image" means manifestation, appearance, or visible form. The word was used to describe a person's portrait or his reflection in the mirror. It was also used to speak of idol images, statues that were intended to express the intangible qualities of pagan deities in tangible form. This important phrase means that Jesus is the visible form of the invisible God.

He is the One who has expressed the intangible qualities of God in tangible form. This description implies His deity, His identity as God in human form. (CQ)

Christ's deity is also mentioned by other biblical writers. John 1:1 says, "In the beginning was the Word, and the Word was with God, and the Word was God." John continued in verse 14 with the words, "The Word became flesh and took up residence among us. We observed His glory, the glory as the One and Only Son from the Father, full of grace and truth." If the Word is God and the Word is Jesus—then Jesus is God. The writer of Hebrews declared, "The Son is the radiance of God's glory and the exact expression of His nature, sustaining all things by His powerful word" (Heb. 1:3). Jesus is not somewhat like God. It's not that He has some "god-like" qualities. Instead, He is "the exact expression of His nature."

Jesus is God. Therefore, all of the attributes and abilities of God are in Christ. If Jesus is God, then is anything impossible for Him? Is there a sickness He cannot heal? Is there a bill He cannot pay? Is there is a problem He cannot fix? Is there a marriage He cannot restore? Jesus is God. When a Christian understands the deity of Christ, there is security.

WORD STUDY

"Fullness" (1:19)

The word translated as "fullness" means the "sum total" or "completeness." The one referred to in the pronoun "His" is clearly "God." The HCSB helps readers properly identify the antecedent by capitalizing the pronoun "His." Thus, Paul is asserting that the sum total or completeness of God dwelled in Christ. The sentence is later clarified by Paul in Colossians 2:9, "For the entire fullness of God's nature dwells bodily in Christ." All that is essential to God's being resided in Jesus in bodily form. Simply put, Jesus is fully God and fully man. Jesus is not partially but completely God. Everything that makes God, God, has made its home in the body of Jesus Christ. (CQ)

2. Jesus is Creator (Col. 1:16).

"For everything was created by Him, in heaven and on earth, the visible and the invisible, whether thrones or dominions or rulers or authorities—all things have been created through Him and for Him."

Jesus is the Creator; He is not an artist. An artist takes what is and makes something beautiful. The Creator speaks to what is not and brings it to be. When we understand Christ as Creator, we can find security in knowing that God is not limited to the resources we have, or the opportunities we see, or the strength we possess. He has so much creative potential within Him that He can speak to the invisible and make it visible.

If you reflect on creation from Genesis 1–2, you will notice that God spoke everything into existence. The creative directive was, "Then God said ... and it was so." By the power of His word He created plants, animals, seas, land, people, planets, stars, solar systems, galaxies, space, time, and matter. Jesus is the Creator. If He created everything by the power of His word, is there any problem too great for His power?

Take Christ's creative power and apply it to your life. When you're concerned about the health of a loved one, remember, Jesus is the Creator. When you're in need of a job, remember, all He has to do is speak a word. When your courage is gone and your faith is wavering and your hope is almost out, remember that Jesus does not need a head start to fix your problem. He can speak your answer into being.

You are secure in Christ.

Left: Creation epic tablet. In this episode the Babylonian god Anshar summons the gods together for a banquet, to celebrate Marduk's appointment as champion of the gods following his defeat of Tiamat, primaeval Chaos. The tall narrow shape is characteristic of tablets in this series.

A CLOSER LOOK

Thrones, dominions, rulers, and authorities (1:16)

While everything was created by Jesus, Colossians 1:16 specifically mentions "thrones," "dominions," "rulers," and "authorities." These designations refer to various ranks of spiritual beings or angels. "Thrones" are apparently the angels that attend to the throne of God in the highest heaven. "Dominions" (literally "bearers of ruling authority") seem to be a class of angels who oversee the government of nations. "Rulers" are the archangels, the generals of the heavenly hosts. "Authorities" are probably angels who have particular powers to perform special tasks. The ancient Jews regarded these classes of angels as the highest and greatest of all. Yet Christ is identified as the Creator of these highest and greatest of angels. This clearly shows that those groups that claim that Jesus was merely an angelic being rather than God in human form greatly insult His dignity. Far more than a mere angel, Jesus created the highest and greatest of angels. He is as superior to the angels as the Creator is to the creature. This truth strengthens the notion that we are secure in Christ. (CQ)

3. Jesus is Ruler (Col. 1:17a).

"He is before all things."

Jesus is not a passive Creator who watches idly; He is the ruler "before all things." He is Lord; He is Sovereign; He is God.

When you pray, keep in mind that you're not just sharing your heart with someone who cares. When you pray, you are sharing your heart with the One who is in charge. Jesus loves you, and He cares for you. We are told to cast all our cares on Him (1 Pet. 5:7). All of that would be encouraging if Jesus was just concerned. However, He can actually do something about the trials you're facing. Jesus is Ruler. Therefore, you are secure in Christ.

4. Jesus is Sustainer (Col. 1:17b).

"by Him all things hold together."

There are so many things that make it possible for life to exist. Dry air is primarily made up of nitrogen (78.09 percent) and oxygen (20.95 percent). The remaining one percent is made up of argon (0.93 percent), carbon dioxide (0.03 percent), and other trace gases (0.003 percent). Those are some pretty specific measurements. Who keeps the mixture in right proportion?

How do the planets know which path to take? How do birds know to fly south in winter? What makes crops grow, and rain fall, and life flourish? Who feeds the animals, churns the seas, and controls the seasons? His name is Jesus. Jesus is the Sustainer. By Him all things hold together.

Sometimes I feel overwhelmed by the responsibilities of being a husband, a father, a pastor, a leader, a neighbor, etc. The issues keep piling up. The problems seem endless. There are great opportunities in every direction. There is so much to do, but I have limited control. There are times when I feel helpless, and I must resign myself to watching from the sidelines.

Jesus has never felt helpless. There has never been a time when He could not wear every hat, juggle every ball, and keep every plate spinning. Day after day, He cares for every need and He knows what to do. Jesus is the Sustainer.

When you feel helpless, run to Jesus! You are secure in Him.

5. Jesus is Head of the church (Col. 1:18a).

"He is also the head of the body, the church."

People may hold leadership positions within the church, but Christ is the Head of the church. The reason I have hope in the future of the church is not because I see every pastor sold out to God or the world embracing Christ's ideals. I have hope for the future of the church because Christ is still the Head.

I have hope for the future of the church because Christ is still the Head.

He will direct the church, position the church, and use the church as He sees fit. Jesus is the Head of the church. As a Christian, you are secure in Him.

6. Jesus is Savior (Col. 1:20).

"and through Him to reconcile everything to Himself by making peace through the blood of His cross—whether things on earth or things in heaven."

Humanity was created for a relationship with God. Sin severed that relationship. If the story of redemption stopped there, life would have no meaning. Praise God, the story keeps going. There was nothing we could do to reconcile the relationship on our own. Instead, Jesus did what we could never do. He lived a perfect life, He died on the cross for our sins, and He rose from the dead that we might have life. He offers eternal life (a reconciled relationship; John 17:3) to those who will repent of their sins by placing faith in Jesus Christ. That is the gospel message.

As Christians, we are secure in Christ because we have been reconciled to God. We don't need to feel like God is mad at us and out to get us. Romans 8:1 says, "Therefore, no condemnation now exists for those in Christ Jesus." We can boldly come before the throne of grace with confidence. We are reconciled to God.

Sleep well tonight. Relish the reconciliation of God. Enjoy the blessing of knowing that Jesus is the Savior, and He has secured your position before God.

Do not fear; you are secure in Christ.

We've listed six aspects of Christ's nature. Do you see how an understanding of Christ's nature brings security to the believer? Your greatest need is not more money, more opportunities, more time, or more ability. Your greatest need is to know Christ, to believe Christ, and to live in fellowship with Christ. You are secure in Christ because He is all you need.

Personal Reflection

1. Where in your life do you struggle with the notion that Christ is all you need? Identify two or three areas.

2. The apostle Paul listed six aspects of Christ's nature in Colossians 1:15-20. Based on what he wrote, why do Christians still struggle with security?

3. Our security is connected to Christ's nature. What are a few practical ways to grow in your knowledge and understanding of Christ's nature?

CHAPTER 2

You Are Reconciled In Christ

COLOSSIANS 1:13-14,20-22a

It was a Sunday morning in 2001. My wife and I had been married about five years, and we were at our first pastorate in North Carolina. When you're a pastor, getting up early on Sunday morning is a necessity. While I've never seen it in a Baptist handbook, I'm pretty sure the ability to finish your fourth cup of coffee by 6 a.m. is a prerequisite for pastoring a Baptist church. At any rate, I was thinking through the messages for the day, and my wife was going over the song she was supposed to sing.

After getting dressed, I sat in the living room, continuing to look over my message. A few minutes later, my wife walked around the corner sporting a new hairdo. Being the sensitive husband that I am, I made an off-the-wall comment about the name of the hairdo. I thought I was being funny; she thought I was being mean.

I have a trivia question for you. What's the last thing your wife wants to hear just before she sings a solo at church? If you guessed, "a criticism of her hair"—you would be correct. Before I knew it, things were less than happy at the Gotthardt house.

I tried to explain that my comment was intended to be funny, and I wasn't trying to hurt her feelings. But once the comment was made, there was no going back. We talked, we argued, we tried to work through it, but the tension kept mounting.

The moment was intensified based on a commitment we made before marriage. We agreed that we would always work through our differences on the spot. If that meant canceling an appointment, being late for work, or stopping whatever we were doing to reconcile our differences—that's what we were going to do.

After 15 to 20 minutes of discussion at home, we needed to drive to church. We continued the conversation in the car. After a 15-minute drive, we arrived at the church. The issue was not resolved. We sat in the car and continued to talk (waving to church members who were walking by). Sunday school started and we were still in the parking lot. The tension of the argument was coupled with the pressure of being on time. We were already late for Sunday school, and we decided to drive around.

After 40 minutes of driving, we finally worked through the argument. I drove back to church as quickly as I could. When we arrived, the music for the morning service had already started. I walked into the service, took my place at the front, and tried to refocus my attention on worshiping God. A few minutes later, my wife sang her solo, I preached the morning message, and life went on. While everything was reconciled, it was probably one of the most stressful mornings of our ministry.

I learned two valuable lessons that morning. First, funny comments about your wife's hairdo are not funny. Second, life has a way of dividing relationships.

In Colossians 1, Paul described a formerly divided relationship that has been reconciled. "Once you were alienated and hostile in your minds because of your evil actions. But now He has reconciled you by His physical body through His death" (1:21-22a). Paul was referring to the relationship between God and those who place faith in Jesus Christ.

The story of relationship is the story of the Bible. Humanity was created for a relationship with God. Sin severed that relationship. There was nothing we could do to reconcile the relationship on our own. Our good works were not enough. Our good intentions fell short. Our attempts to keep the law failed. However, Jesus did what we could never do. He lived a sinless life. He died on the cross for our sins. He rose from the dead that we might have life. Finally, God offers eternal life to those who will repent of their sins by placing faith in Jesus Christ. That is the essence of the gospel message.

Many Christians would agree with everything they just read. But before you accept that description and move on, I want you to really think about the term *eternal life*. What is eternal life?

The vast majority of Christians define eternal life as going to heaven when they die. Ironically, that is not the way Jesus defined eternal life. In John 17:3, Jesus said, "This is eternal life: that they may know You, the only true God, and the One You have sent—Jesus Christ." Eternal life is to know God.

This verse is like the Rosetta Stone for so much of God's activity. When we understand eternal life, it puts much of God's activity in perspective. The reason Christ set aside the glory of heaven and came to earth is so we could know God. The purpose of Christ's death on the cross was so we could know God. Romans 6:23 says, "For the wages of sin is death, but the gift of God is eternal life in Christ Jesus our Lord." Based on John 17:3, we know that God's gift is the opportunity to know Him.

Unfortunately, many Christians have never made the connection between eternal life and knowing God. They thought eternal life was going to a place called heaven when they die. Heaven is great, but heaven is a benefit of knowing God—it's not the main gift. God's primary gift is Himself. We were created for a relationship with God, sin severed that relationship, and Jesus died and rose again to reconcile the relationship. It's all about relationship.

Unfortunately, many Christians have never made the connection between eternal life and knowing God.

As a Christian, you are reconciled in Christ. The primary emphasis in Colossians is that Christ is all we need. Being reconciled to God is one facet of that truth. Jesus is the only means of reconciliation, and Paul taught this truth in multiple letters. Notice the emphasis placed on reconciliation.

- To believers in Rome, Paul said, "For if, while we were enemies, we were reconciled to God through the death of His Son, then how much more, having been reconciled, will we be saved by His life!" (Rom. 5:10)

- To those in Corinth, Paul said, "Everything is from God, who reconciled us to Himself through Christ and gave us the ministry of reconciliation: That is, in Christ, God was reconciling the world to Himself, not counting their trespasses against them, and He has committed the message of reconciliation to us" (2 Cor. 5:18-19).

- To those in Colossae, Paul declared, "Once you were alienated and hostile in your minds because of your evil actions. But now He has reconciled you by His physical body through His death" (Col. 1:21-22a).

You are reconciled to God in Christ. Reconciliation is a freeing concept. However, what does it really mean to be reconciled to God? In Colossians, Paul described the depth of reconciliation in several verses.

1. You were rescued and transferred (Col. 1:13).

"He has rescued us from the domain of darkness and transferred us into the kingdom of the Son He loves."

The visual picture that corresponds with this verse is incredible. The word *rescued* means "to draw to oneself." At salvation,

God drew us to Himself. He rescued us from Satan and his domain of darkness. The word *domain* can be translated "power," "jurisdiction," or "authority." God has drawn us to Himself by pulling us away from the power, jurisdiction, or authority of darkness.

Notice that the word *rescued* in verse 13 is past tense. It describes a completed action. Our deliverance was not gradual; it was instantaneous. As Christians, we don't need God to rescue us from sin and Satan; He already has done that. We need to live like those who are free. "Christ has liberated us to be free. Stand firm then and don't submit again to a yoke of slavery" (Gal. 5:1).

It would be amazing enough if God just freed us from Satan's domain. But Christ went beyond freedom to inclusion.

Think of America's past roles in liberating people who suffered under the tyranny of a dictator or an oppressive government. It's one thing to overthrow an oppressive power and liberate people. That's incredible. It's another thing to make the formerly oppressed citizens of America. Verse 13 teaches that God liberated us from Satan's power, jurisdiction, and authority. He also "transferred us into the kingdom of the Son He loves." To transfer means "to remove or change." God removed us from darkness and He immersed us in light. Paul wrote of this change in 2 Corinthians 5:17. "Therefore, if anyone is in Christ, he is a new creation; old things have passed away, and look, new things have come."

LEARNING ACTIVITY

Not Just "From" but "To"

Those who have been reconciled to God in Christ were not only delivered from something but also to something. Drawing upon Paul's example in Colossians 1:13, list some other "from/to" descriptors of those in Christ.

Rescued from...
"the domain of darkness" (v. 13)

Transferred to...
"the kingdom of His Son" (v. 13)

Take a moment and personalize these teachings. Based on the truths of Colossians 1:13, does sin have power over you? Are you helpless in temptation? Is the real struggle in breaking free? Or is the real struggle in believing God? Scripture says, "He has rescued us from the domain of darkness and transferred us into the kingdom of the Son He loves."

What does it mean to be reconciled to God? It means you were rescued from the power of sin and transferred to the kingdom of Christ.

2. You have forgiveness of your sins in Him (Col. 1:14).

"We have redemption, the forgiveness of sins, in Him."

The first part of this statement seems familiar. At salvation, Jesus forgives our sins. We emphasize, sing about, and preach the wonders of Christ's forgiveness.

Below: Funerary relief of Cyzique, Turkey. The servants of the deceased are depicted smaller than their masters.

Where is Forgiveness Found?

People look for forgiveness in...

- The hope that good deeds outweigh bad ones
- Their affiliation with a church
- Their sincerity of heart
- Other:

It's the last part of that statement that is unfamiliar to many. "We have redemption, the forgiveness of sins, in Him." Our redemption is *in Him*. Our forgiveness is *in Him*. What does it mean to be in Him?

"In Him" (v. 14) speaks of our position and our identity. As Christians, we are in Christ, and Christ is in us. Jesus said in John 15:4, "Remain in Me, and I in you. Just as a branch is unable to produce fruit by itself unless it remains on the vine, so neither can you unless you remain in Me." Paul told believers in Colossae:

> So if you have been raised with the Messiah, seek what is above, where the Messiah is, seated at the right hand of God. Set your minds on what is above, not on what is on the earth. For you have died, and your life is hidden with the Messiah in God (Col. 3:1-3).

We are positioned in Christ, we are raised with Christ, we are seated with Christ, and our life is hidden in Christ. Our position and our identity are found in Christ. He is our life.

A CLOSER LOOK

"In Him" in Colossians

- To the saints *in Christ* at Colossae (1:2).
- We have heard of your faith *in Christ Jesus* (1:4).
- We have redemption, the forgiveness of sins, *in Him* (1:14).
- For God was pleased to have all His fullness dwell *in Him* (1:19).
- We proclaim Him, warning and teaching everyone with all wisdom, so that we may present everyone mature *in Christ* (1:28).

- All the treasures of wisdom and knowledge are hidden *in Him* (2:3).
- Therefore, as you have received Christ Jesus the Lord, walk *in Him*, rooted and built up *in Him* (2:6-7).
- For the entire fullness of God's nature dwells bodily *in Christ* (2:9).
- You were also circumcised *in Him* (2:11).
- For you have died and your life is hidden with the Messiah *in God* (3:3).
- *In Christ* there is not Greek and Jew, circumcision and uncircumcision, barbarian, Scythian, slave and free; but Christ is all and in all (3:11).
- Wives, be submissive to your husbands, as is fitting *in the Lord* (3:18).
- Tychicus, our dearly loved brother, faithful servant, and fellow slave *in the Lord* (4:7).
- Pay attention to the ministry you have received *in the Lord* (4:17).

Oddly enough, our life began with His death. Jesus died a substitutionary death for us. His death paid our sin debt. Romans 6:23 says, "For the wages of sin is death." Wages are what we earn for what we've done. The Bible indicates that death is what we earned for our sin. The reason Jesus died was to pay the penalty for our sin. When the penalty was paid, reconciliation was possible.

When a person repents of sin by placing faith in Jesus Christ, God gives that person a new identity. I am no longer "Paul, the sinner separated from God." I am "Paul, the saint who is reconciled in Christ." My life is in Christ. He is my identity.

In Him, we have a new identity and position before God.

WORD STUDY
"Redemption" (1:14)

Redemption refers to the payment of a price either to free someone from slavery or to ransom them from a sentence for a crime. Jesus redeems believers in both senses. However, the

latter of the two nuances is the one that Paul has in mind in Colossians 1:14. Paul defined this redemption as "the forgiveness of sins." Forgiveness entailed erasing the record of a person's sins. This record would provide the list of charges and the supporting evidence to prosecute the sinner in final judgment (Col. 2:13-14). Once that record was erased, all charges against the accused were dropped. Consequently, the heavenly Judge would slam His gavel and pronounce the defendant, "Not guilty!" For this reason, Jesus would present believers to the Father in judgment "blameless before Him" (Col. 1:22). (CQ)

3. You are at peace with God (Col. 1:20).

"and through Him to reconcile everything to Himself by making peace through the blood of His cross—whether things on earth or things in heaven."

In the opening illustration, my wife and I needed to restore peace between us. We needed to reconcile. We could have postponed reconciliation, showed up at church and acted like nothing was wrong. But in our hearts we could not worship God while being at odds with one another. Broken fellowship is distracting. Peace comes through reconciliation.

Paul told the Colossian believers that Christ made peace with God "through the blood of His cross." His death secured our peace. As a Christian, you are not at war with God. God is not waiting for the right moment to zap you for everything you've done wrong. You have been forgiven. Psalm 103:12 says, "As far as the east is from the west, so far has He removed our transgressions from us." Every sin you have committed and every sin you will commit were forgiven at the cross. You are completely forgiven. The fullness of forgiveness is why Paul declared, "Therefore, no condemnation now exists for those in Christ Jesus" (Rom. 8:1). Why is there no condemnation? Because you are "in Christ Jesus."

You are forgiven in Christ. You are at peace with God.

4. Christ initiated and pursued a relationship with you (Col. 1:21-22a).

"Once you were alienated and hostile in your minds because of your evil actions. But now He has reconciled you by His physical body through His death."

When I was in elementary and middle school, it was not uncommon for love notes to be passed in class. Most of them were the same. "I like you. Do you like me? Check yes or no." If you sent the note, you hoped the other person checked "yes."

As strange as it sounds, the gospel is God's love note to you. God is saying, "I love you. Do you love Me? Check yes or no." The incredible truth of the gospel is that God initiated the relationship. He sent the love note to you. He pursued you. Paul said, "You were alienated ... but now He has reconciled you." God took the initiative. As Christians, we did not reconcile ourselves to God. God called us, He quickened our dead spirit, He enabled us to understand the gospel, and He made reconciliation possible. God pursued you and me.

The incredible truth of the gospel is that God initiated the relationship.

It is wonderful to know that you are reconciled to God. It is even more astounding to realize that He initiated that reconciliation. Christ initiated and pursued a relationship with you.

Left: Slave market in ancient Thagaste (Souk Ahras, Algeria). The word "redemption" (1:14) came from a root word meaning "to purchase from the slave market.

What does it mean to be reconciled to God through Christ? In just a few verses, we've seen that...

- You were rescued and transferred (1:13).
- You have forgiveness of sins in Him (1:14).
- You are at peace with God (1:20).
- Christ initiated and pursued a relationship with you (1:21-22a).

Each of the four statements speaks to what Christ has done for us. In chapter one, we found that Christ is all we need to be secure in life. In chapter two, we've seen that Christ is all we need to be reconciled to God.

Are you worried and anxious? Are you scrambling for stability and hope? Are your days filled with regrets and your nights consumed with guilt from the past? Colossians shares good news. You are forgiven. You are reconciled. Sin's power has been broken. God has pursued you through the corridors of time. A new life is yours because you are in Christ. Paul was right. Christ is all you need.

A CLOSER LOOK
Who Are You?

We have a new identity in Christ. We need to see ourselves as God sees us. This list describes who you are from God's perspective.

- You are the salt of the earth and the light of the world (Matt. 5:13-14).
- You are a child of God (part of His family) (John 1:12; Rom. 8:16).
- You are part of the true Vine (John 15:1,5).
- You are Christ's friend (John 15:15).
- You are chosen and appointed by Christ to bear His fruit (John 15:16).
- You are a witness of Christ (Acts 1:8).
- You are a slave of righteousness (Rom. 6:18).
- You are a child of God (Rom. 8:14, 15; Gal. 3:26; 4:6).
- You are a joint-heir with Christ (Rom. 8:17).
- You are a temple of God (1 Cor. 3:16; 6:19).
- You are joined to the Lord (1 Cor. 6:17).
- You are a member of Christ's body (1 Cor. 12:27; Eph. 5:30).
- You are a new creation (2 Cor. 5:17).
- You are reconciled to God and a minister of reconciliation (2 Cor. 5:18-19).
- You are a son of God and one in Christ (Gal. 3:26,28).
- You are a saint (Eph. 1:1; 1 Cor. 1:2; Phil. 1:1, Col. 1:2).
- You are God's workmanship (Eph. 2:10).

- You are a fellow citizen with the rest of God's people (Eph. 2:19).
- You are a prisoner of Christ (Eph. 3:1; 4:1).
- You are righteous and holy (Eph. 4:24).
- You are a citizen of heaven and seated in heaven right now (Phil. 3:20; Eph. 2:6).
- You are hidden with Christ in God (Col. 3:3).
- You are an expression of the life of Christ (Col. 3:4).
- You are chosen of God, holy, and dearly loved (Col. 3:12; 1 Thess. 1:4).
- You are a son of light and not of darkness (1 Thess. 5:5).
- You are a holy brother, partaker of a heavenly calling (Heb. 3:1).
- You are a partaker of Christ (Heb. 3:14).
- You are one of God's living stones (1 Pet. 2:5).
- You are a chosen race, a royal priesthood, a holy nation (1 Pet. 2:9-10).
- You are an alien and stranger to this world (1 Pet. 2:11).
- You are an enemy of the devil (1 Pet. 5:8),
- You are now a child of God (1 John 3:1-2),
- You are born of God and the evil one (the Devil) can't touch you (1 John 5:18),
- You are a sheep of His pasture. You have everything you need (Pss. 23; 100),

Personal Reflection

1. Jesus defined "eternal life" as knowing God. What are some practical ways you can grow in your knowledge of God? What can you do to incorporate these practices into daily life?

2. Satan likes to remind us of our failures and shortcomings. As Christians, our sins have been forgiven (past, present, and future). Make a list of the sins that Satan uses against you. Once you complete your list, read Colossians 1:14 and Romans 8:1. Claim the promises of Scripture over those areas. Spend time with God and that list. Trust God when He says, "You are forgiven."

3. You are a new creation in Christ (2 Cor. 5:17). Review "A Closer Look: Who Are You?" What part of your new identity do you have the most difficulty accepting? What keeps you from accepting all of your new identity?

CHAPTER 3

You Are Complete In Christ

COLOSSIANS 1:22,27-28; 2:2-3,9-10

I have a confession to make. I am a fan of unofficial surveys. I know that confession is not going to make the cover of the tabloids, but here's what I mean. There is something to be said for unbridled honesty. While the structure and sterility of test groups are necessary for some types of research, they can be cumbersome for others. When people know their answers are "official," they tend to overthink things. They give responses that are expected or responses that seem right (regardless of truth). Sometimes the best responses are off the cuff.

For curiosity sake, I typed the following question into a search engine: What makes you feel complete? Apparently, I was not the only person conducting an unofficial survey. Several sites asked similar questions, "What completes you, what do you need to be complete, what makes you complete?" The following list is a summary of the primary responses to those questions.

- The love of my family
- Knowing that someone feels the same way I do
- My Creator and Redeemer
- My friends
- Changing someone's life
- Helping others
- Giving
- Knowing I'm loved
- Entertaining family and friends
- Praying
- Knowing that someone needs me
- Communicating with Jesus
- My soul mate
- Making great meals
- Spending time in nature
- Spiritual pursuits

While I didn't have time to read every answer on every site, I did read most of the answers on the top sites. I noticed a few trends. I didn't see any mention of money, jobs, education, possessions, power, or fame. I find that ironic. Society encourages us to pursue those things to be complete; however, people do not list those things as the source of what makes them complete.

Another trend I noticed was the emphasis placed on relationships. Of the 16 responses listed above, 13 are relationally centered. This discovery makes sense in light of Scripture. Humanity was created for relationship. We were created for relationship with God and with each other. It only makes sense that we find completion within the context of our design.

So let me ask you the same question. What makes you feel complete? Maybe a more personal question would be this: Are you complete?

There is a really good chance that your answers will be similar to the ones listed by others. The joy of family, friends, giving, and serving will bring a level of fulfillment. However, before you finalize your response, I want you to see the apostle Paul's answer to those questions. Paul addressed the subject of completeness with believers in Colossae. While the entire section (Col. 1:22–2:10) is important for context, I've selected a few key verses (Col. 1:22,27-28; 2:2-3,9-10). Words and phrases have been italicized for emphasis.

> "But now He has *reconciled* you by His physical body through His death, to present you *holy, faultless,* and *blameless* before Him" (1:22).

> "God wanted to make known among the Gentiles the glorious wealth of this mystery, which is *Christ in you,* the *hope* of glory. We proclaim Him, warning and teaching everyone with all wisdom, so that we may present everyone *mature* in Christ" (1:27-28).

> "I want their hearts to be *encouraged* and *joined together in love,* so that they may have all the riches of assured understanding and have the knowledge of God's mystery—Christ. All the treasures of wisdom and knowledge are hidden in Him" (2:2-3).

> "For the entire *fullness* of God's nature dwells bodily in Christ, and you have been *filled* by Him, who is the head over every ruler and authority" (2:9-10).

In chapter one, I shared some of the heretical teachings that attacked the first century church. At the center of the controversy was the sufficiency of Christ. Is Christ enough for salvation? Is He enough to sustain you, develop you, and keep you? Paul's answer was clear. Christ is enough. In the passages above, Paul described how Christ is not only enough—He is everything. Our lives are complete in Him.

Notice the words and phrases that were italicized: *reconciled, holy, faultless, blameless, Christ in you, hope, mature, encouraged, joined together in love, fullness,* and *filled.* The whole section is relevant, but Colossians 2:10 is key: "And you have been filled by Him." The New American Standard Bible translates that statement like this: "and in Him you have been made complete." Let's put the pieces together.

In Christ, you have been reconciled to God. Our supreme purpose in creation has become a reality. As Christians, we are seen by God through Christ. We are holy because He is holy (1 Pet. 2:9). We are faultless and blameless because Christ is faultless and blameless. Our life is in Christ and Christ is in us (Col. 3:3; Gal. 2:20). Therefore, you have hope, you are mature, you can be encouraged, you are joined together in love, you experience the fullness of God's nature, and you are filled by Him.

How would you describe someone who is fulfilling his or her created purpose, is faultless and blameless, hopeful, mature, encouraged, joined with others in love, and completely filled with the nature of God? Paul described that person as "complete in Him."

If you are a Christian, that describes you. You are complete in Christ. That does not mean that other outside relationships, accomplishments, and opportunities do not bring a certain amount of joy and fulfillment. God has a tendency to bless us with more than we deserve. However, if the only relationship you have is Christ, and if the only encouragement you have is Christ, and if the only hope you have is Christ—you are still complete.

Think for a moment about the implications of that statement. If all you have is Christ, you are still complete.

If all you have is Christ, you are still complete.

How many Christians are chasing someone or something to make them complete? How many Christian teenagers pursue the wrong crowd, make poor decisions, and gravitate to sex and drugs in an effort to feel whole? Think about the Christian marriages that are torn apart because one or both spouses thinks a career makes them complete. In every corner of society, in every walk of life, people are clamoring for completeness. Let Paul's voice penetrate the confusion. "In Him you have been made complete."

Let's dig deeper. What does it look like to be complete in Christ?

1. You are completely purified in Christ (Col. 1:22).

"But now He has reconciled you by His physical body through His death, to present you holy, faultless, and blameless before Him."

Our reconciliation with God came through the death of Christ on the cross. In chapter two, we found that being reconciled to God means...

- You were rescued and transferred (1:13).
- You have forgiveness of sins in Him (1:14).
- You are at peace with God (1:20).
- Christ initiated and pursued a relationship with you (1:21-22a).

The reality of reconciliation is the foundation for completeness. It is due to Christ's death on the cross that He can present us "holy, faultless, and blameless before Him." Here's a quick breakdown of those three words.

- *Holy* means separated unto God.
- *Faultless* means to be without blemish or spot.
- *Blameless* means to be free from blemish and from the charge of it.

We are separated unto God, without blemish, and without the charge of former blemishes. Your slate has been wiped clean. Your sins are forgiven. In God's eyes, you are holy. As Christians, we are completely purified in Christ.

WORD STUDY

"Blameless" (1:22)

The word *blameless* is a legal term that means "not susceptible to indictment," "free from accusation." "Holy, faultless, and blameless" are practically synonymous in this context and express the legal standing that the believer will have when he is presented to the court on Judgment Day. Because of Jesus' sacrificial death, when the divine

Judge slams His gavel and pronounces His verdict, He will shout, "Not guilty!" Paul was clearly describing the doctrine of "justification," in which believers are considered righteous, despite their sinfulness, because Jesus paid the penalty that their sins deserved (Rom. 3:21–4:5). (CQ)

2. You have complete hope because Christ is in you (Col. 1:27).

"God wanted to make known among the Gentiles the glorious wealth of this mystery, which is Christ in you, the hope of glory."

In middle school, there were a lot of inside jokes and gossip. One person would say, "Have you heard about so-and-so?" The other person might say, "I haven't heard anything." The reply was often, "If you don't know, I can't tell you." At that, the instigator would walk off feeling superior and the other person would walk away feeling left out.

The power of the instigator was in the illusion of secret knowledge. In verse 27, God lets New Testament believers in on a secret. It wasn't an inside joke or frivolous gossip. The secret that was hidden from Old Testament saints is "Christ in you, the hope of glory."

WORD STUDY
"Mystery" (1:27)

The word *mystery* does not refer to a puzzle that human beings can solve on their own if they are clever enough. In the Old Testament, a "mystery" refers to aspects of God's plan for the future that are known only to God, until He graciously chooses to reveal them (Dan. 2:18-19,27,29-30,47). The mystery to which Paul referred was an aspect of God's plan that would be accomplished through the Messiah, Jesus Christ, which was hidden from God's people in the past, but had been revealed to Paul and proclaimed through him to many others. (CQ)

In the Old Testament, Messiah's arrival was predicted. He would usher Israel into a time of prosperity and peace. He would lead His people, teach His people, and embolden His people. However, no one could have predicted that Messiah would actually live in His people. The indwelling Messiah was a secret.

How does that secret apply to you and me? First, Christ is in you. You don't have to hope that God will draw near; He cannot get any closer. He's in you. Second, the indwelling reality of Christ is our hope. Our hope is not in government, people, churches, programs, or strategies. Christ in you is "the hope of glory."

You don't need something else to give you hope; you have complete hope because Christ is in you.

Our hope is not in government, people, churches, programs, or strategies.

---

3. You are on the path to complete maturity in Christ (Col. 1:28).

"We proclaim Him, warning and teaching everyone with all wisdom, so that we may present everyone mature in Christ."

Paul wants to present believers as mature in Christ. How does that happen? The answer is found in the first three words: "We proclaim Him." It's great to teach about faith, love, grace, and giving. All of those subjects are biblical and necessary. However, if those concepts are not linked to the proclamation of Christ, we've missed the mark.

When addressing the church in Corinth, Paul said, "For I didn't think it was a good idea to know anything among you except Jesus Christ and Him crucified" (1 Cor. 2:2). On the surface, it would seem that Paul's preaching would be too narrowly defined. He wanted to know Christ and Him crucified. What about faith, grace, love, peace, the spiritual disciplines, missions, etc.? Was Paul refusing to grow in those areas? Not even close! Paul understood that every facet of the Christian life becomes a reality when Christ lives through us (Gal. 2:20). Therefore, when we proclaim Christ and people pursue Christ—He will live these aspects through us.

Every facet of the Christian life becomes a reality when Christ lives through us.

Paul's proclamation of Christ had two parts, one negative and one positive. He spoke of "warning and teaching." Warning is counsel related to sin and impending punishment. Teaching refers to truth for encouragement and development. Both must be done with all wisdom.

When Christ is proclaimed (through warning and instruction), you are on the path to complete maturity in Christ.

4. You are strengthened by unity in Christ (Col. 2:2).

"I want their hearts to be encouraged and joined together in love, so that they may have all the riches of assured understanding and have the knowledge of God's mystery—Christ."

The truths Paul shared were intended to encourage the Colossian believers and to join them together in love. The word "encourage" means "to call alongside." It was a word used to exhort, comfort, encourage, and strengthen.

The phrase "joined together in love" describes a deeply held unity. Just as the human body is joined together by what every joint supplies (Eph. 4:16; Col. 2:19), Christians are joined together in love. We share a common life. The indwelling reality of Christ brings us together in love. It gives a point of commonality and union.

You are not alone; you are strengthened by unity in Christ.

5. You have all wisdom and knowledge in Christ (Col. 2:3).

"All the treasures of wisdom and knowledge are hidden in Him."

There comes a time when most people embark on a quest for knowledge, wisdom, and truth. It's a part of maturing. Teenagers question authority. College students explore knowledge. Adults weed through information to settle on convictions. Each group tries to move past the pat answers and go to the source. What do I believe? Why do I believe it?

At the end of our quest for knowledge, wisdom, and truth—we find Christ. "All the treasures of wisdom and knowledge are hidden in Him." Jesus added to this idea in John 14:6, when He said, "I am the way, the truth, and the life."

Pursuing wisdom, knowledge, and truth are as simple as pursuing Christ. He is the source. You have all wisdom and knowledge in Christ.

6. You have been completely filled by Christ (Col. 2:9-10a).

"For the entire fullness of God's nature dwells bodily in Christ, and you have been filled by Him."

Verse 9 speaks of the deity of Christ. Jesus was not just a great man with "godlike" qualities. Jesus is God, and "the entire fullness of God's nature dwells bodily in Christ." How does Christ's nature impact you?

To fill means to take up all the space, close a hole, or meet a need. Paul said, "You have been filled by Him." Every need you have, He has already filled. Paul told believers in Ephesus that they had every spiritual blessing in Christ (Eph. 1:3). How can we have every spiritual blessing? How can Christ fill every need? The fullness of God dwells in Christ, and you are filled by Christ.

The fullness of God dwells in Christ, and you are filled by Christ.

This concept is almost staggering. The Creator of this universe has chosen to make His abode in you (John 14:23). Infinite resides in finite. God does not promise to be around, help occasionally, or check in when needed. He promises to be with us and in us (Matt. 28:20; John 14:17).

You have been completely filled by Christ.

What does a Christian need to be complete? Absolutely nothing! When you have Christ, you have it all. You are complete in Christ.

When you have Christ, you have it all.

When will Jesus be enough? That question is central to being complete in Christ. As Christians, we are constantly pursuing the next big thing. We chase after the next Bible study, Christian conference, best-selling book, or insight from God. In Philippians 3:5-11, Paul listed his impressive credentials and accomplishments. Yet he counted them as loss for the surpassing value of knowing Christ. In Philippians 3:10 he revealed his greatest desire: "to know Him." Jesus was enough for Paul. Is He enough for you?

A CLOSER LOOK

The Concept of Fullness in Colossians

Paul used the Greek word *pleroma* numerous times in Colossians. (These are underlined below.) The word *pleroma* communicates the idea of "fullness" or "completion." At times, this completion is God's work (1:9,19; 2:9-10) while other usages indicate human responsibility (1:24-25;4:17).

1:9	<u>filled</u> with the knowledge of His will
1:19	all His <u>fullness</u> to dwell in Him
1:24	<u>completing</u> in my flesh
1:25	make God's message <u>fully</u> known
2:2	<u>assured</u> understanding
2:9	entire <u>fullness</u> of God's nature
2:10	you have been <u>filled</u> by Him
4:12	<u>fully</u> assured in everything God wills
4:17	so that you can <u>accomplish</u> it

Personal Reflection

1. What have you been chasing to feel complete?

2. Knowing truth and applying truth are two different things. You are complete in Christ. How does knowing you are complete in Christ impact the way you live daily?

CHAPTER 4

You Have a New Nature In Christ

COLOSSIANS 2:11-15; 3:9-10

Maybe you've heard the following illustration. While serving in a remote village in Africa, a missionary witnessed two dogs fighting. The smaller dog was aggressive and dominant; the bigger dog was lethargic and timid. Each time the dogs fought, the smaller dog subdued the larger dog.

The missionary was puzzled. Was the smaller dog that good? Was it bred for fighting? How did the smaller dog continue to win? Curiosity got the best of the missionary. He asked the village chief, "Why does the smaller dog always win?" The chief replied, "It all depends on which dog you feed."

That illustration has been used countless times by pastors and teachers to answer the question, "Why do Christians continue to sin?" It has been suggested that Christians sin because they have two conflicting natures. They received a sin nature at birth, and they received Christ's nature at salvation. The premise has been simple. If you feed Christ's nature, you walk in victory. If you feed the sin nature, you suffer in defeat. Christians continue to sin because they feed the sin nature, and they starve Christ's nature.

It makes sense right? The idea seems logical and spiritual and simple. Why else would a person who loves God continue to sin?

I have an answer that may be uncomfortable for a lot of Christians. It's not neatly packaged, and I don't have a great dog illustration to support it. However, I believe Scripture validates the answer, and it has the capacity to bring incredible freedom to your life.

Why do Christians continue to sin? Christians continue to sin because they live according to the patterns of the old nature and not according to the reality of their new nature in Christ.

The answer does not seem offensive on the surface. Here's the controversial part. The answer is rooted in the belief that Christians do not have two natures; we only have one. We have the nature of Christ.

Why Do Christians Continue to Sin?

Which of the following best answers the question, "Why do Christians continue to sin even after their conversion?"

___ Because the old nature simultaneously exists with the new nature

___ Because justification is progressive and a person can never know for sure they are saved unless they continue in godliness (good works) to the end of their lifetime

___ Because of an ongoing battle with the flesh, the residual habits and mindset developed prior to salvation while living with a sin nature

___ Because they were never genuinely saved in the first place

In this chapter we are discussing the new nature you have in Christ. To grasp its significance, let's spend a few moments discussing the concept of nature. Webster defines nature as "the essential character of something; inborn character or disposition." Pigs enjoy filth because it is in their nature. Chickens cluck because it is in their nature. Fish swim because it is in their nature. Some Bible-believing Christians advocate a two-nature position to describe why Christians sin. In other words, we sin because it is in our nature to sin.

I believe Scripture teaches that believers have one nature, not two. When unbelievers sin, they do so because it is in their nature. They do not have the nature of Christ. When believers sin, it is not because they are bound by their old nature; rather, they are living according to patterns of their old nature.

According to the Bible, when a person enters a relationship with Christ there is an immediate change. He or she died to the old nature (Rom. 6:1-11; Col. 3:3) and became "a new creation" (2 Cor. 5:17). The old person no longer exists. God does not give an *additional* nature; He gives a *new* nature.

The old nature describes the person's position of being separated from God in sin. Every person is born into Adam at birth. Subsequently, every person is born into a sin nature and separated relationally from God. When

Christ saves a person, the individual is said to be *in Christ*. Paul said, "Or are you unaware that all of us who were baptized into Christ Jesus were baptized into His death?" (Rom. 6:3).

Bill Gillham writes, "God had no plan for joining His Holy Spirit to any person's old sin nature. He had no plan to give birth to spiritual Siamese twins who are half spirit-child of Satan through Adam and half spirit-child of God through Christ."[1] It is impossible for a person to be in Adam and in Christ at the same time. Richard Melick writes: "The old self and new self are never described as coexisting in anyone. One replaces the other. ... A believer is a totally new person."[2]

In 2 Corinthians 5:17, the Greek phrase translated "have passed away" is in the perfective aorist tense indicating the finality of the action. The phrase "have come" is in the perfect indicative active tense indicating the continuing state or condition. When taken together, it describes the finality of the old nature in Adam and the continuing awareness of the new nature in Christ.

Why does any of this matter? If Christians think they are still in Adam, they will live, argue, and think from the position of the old nature. They will try to conquer their sin nature and make excuses for why they fail. However, the Bible never teaches Christians to deal with the sin nature. Christ has already dealt with the sin nature at salvation. Martyn Lloyd-Jones said, "We are never called to crucify our old man. Why? Because it has already happened—the old man was crucified with Christ on the cross. Nowhere does the Scripture call upon you to crucify your old man ... for the obvious reason that he has already gone."[3] Instead of addressing the old nature, the Bible tells believers to renew their mind and stop living according to the flesh (Rom. 12:2; 7:18; Gal. 5:16-26). Christians need to see themselves as God sees them.

At this point, our new nature in Christ should be clear. However, if Christians are going to learn to live according to the new nature, we need to address the subject of the flesh. What is the flesh?

Paul described our battle as one between the Spirit and the flesh.

For some Christians, the word "flesh" is synonymous with the old man, the sin nature, or being in Adam. The Greek word for flesh is *sarx*. It can refer either to the physical flesh or to any attempt to fulfill a need or desire apart from Christ. "I say then, walk by the Spirit and you will not carry out the desire of the flesh" (Gal. 5:16). Paul described various manifestations of the flesh. "Now the works of the flesh are obvious: sexual immorality, moral impurity, promiscuity, idolatry, sorcery, hatreds, strife, jealousy, outbursts of anger, selfish ambitions, dissensions, factions, envy, drunkenness, carousing, and anything similar" (Gal. 5:19-21a). In each example, it is an attempt to please self, satisfy self, indulge self, empower self, justify self, defend self, etc. Whenever we attempt to fill a need or desire apart from Christ, it flows from the flesh and results in sin. In Galatians 5:16-18, Paul described our battle as one between the Spirit and the flesh. He did not describe it as a battle between two natures.

For those in Christ, the state of the old nature is clear in Scripture:

- "For we know that our old self was crucified with Him in order that sin's dominion over the body may be abolished, so that we may no longer be enslaved to sin" (Rom. 6:6).

- "I have been crucified with Christ and I no longer live, but Christ lives in me" (Gal. 2:19b-20a).

- "For you have died, and your life is hidden with the Messiah in God" (Col. 3:3).

Who died? Who was crucified with Christ? What did Paul mean when he said, "I no longer live?" If the sin nature is still alive, a lot of passages do not make sense. The battle of the believer is not the battle of conforming the sin nature into righteousness; the real battle is renewing our mind in our new nature in Christ.

The battle of the believer is not the battle of conforming the sin nature into righteousness; the real battle is renewing our mind in our new nature in Christ.

When Christians settle the issue of nature, they are ready to step into a new world of victory, freedom, and understanding. It is not that the person changes his or her position before God; rather, the individual recognizes the position that Christ already has given believers. They are no longer enslaved to sin. They have a new nature.

Based on what you just read, let's look at the way God transitions us into this new nature. Colossians 2:11-15 and 3:9-10 describes both the process and the outcome.

²:¹¹You were also circumcised in Him with a circumcision not done with hands, by putting off the body of flesh, in the circumcision of the Messiah. ¹²Having been buried with Him in baptism, you were also raised with Him through faith in the working of God, who raised Him from the dead. ¹³And when you were dead in trespasses and in the uncircumcision of your flesh, He made you alive with Him and forgave us all our trespasses. ¹⁴He erased the certificate of debt, with its obligations, that was against us and opposed to us, and has taken it out of the way by nailing it to the cross. ¹⁵He disarmed the rulers and authorities and disgraced them publicly; He triumphed over them by Him.

³:⁹Do not lie to one another, since you have put off the old self with its practices ¹⁰and have put on the new self. You are being renewed in knowledge according to the image of your Creator.

How did God transform us into this new nature?

1. Your new nature came through spiritual circumcision by Christ (Col. 2:11).

"You were also circumcised in Him with a circumcision not done with hands, by putting off the body of flesh, in the circumcision of the Messiah."

Remember the context of the church in Colossae. There was a mixture of Gentiles and Jews. Each group brought remnants of their former lives into the church. This section would specifically speak to the beliefs of Jewish legalists.

Jewish boys were circumcised eight days after birth (Lev. 12:2-3). According to Genesis 17:10-14, circumcision indicated that a child belonged to the covenant people. Some Jews believed that circumcision was enough for salvation because it granted membership in the covenant nation. Others believed it was an outward sign to remind people of the need for spiritual cleansing.

In this context, Colossians 2:11 helps us see that the physical act of circumcision is spiritually unnecessary because we have been circumcised spiritually by Christ. Christ is all you need. Instead of cutting away a part of flesh, Christ has cut away the sin nature. "You were also circumcised in Him with a circumcision not done with hands, by putting off the body of flesh, in the circumcision of the Messiah" (Col. 2:11).

The significance of this act is found in Romans 6:6. "For we know that our old self was crucified with Him in order that sin's dominion over the body may be abolished, so that we may no longer be enslaved to sin." When Christ cut away the sin nature, He also cut away sin's dominion. Therefore, you are no longer enslaved to sin. Your new nature came through spiritual circumcision by Christ.

A CLOSER LOOK

"In Him"

The phrases "in Him," "with Him," and "with Christ" express the truth that believers share a special union with Christ that involves them in His experiences. Because of this union, when Christ died, the believer died. When Christ was buried, the believer was buried. When Christ was raised, the believer was raised. Even though the believer has not yet experienced physical death, burial, and resurrection, by his union with Christ he has experienced a spiritual death, burial, and resurrection. Paul will remind believers in Colossians 2:20 that "you died with Christ." When the believer died, "you put off the old man with his practices" (Col. 3:9). The believer experienced an amazing transformation that Paul described as a spiritual circumcision. (CQ)

2. Your new nature came through identification with Christ (Col. 2:12).

"Having been buried with Him in baptism, you were also raised with Him through faith in the working of God, who raised Him from the dead."

Whose nature did you receive? You received the nature of Christ. "I have been crucified with Christ and I no longer live, but Christ lives in me" (Gal. 2:19b-20a). Think back to our

Left: Flint dagger of Gebel al-Arak, an ancient city of upper Egypt. The ivory handle from the tooth of a hippopotamus is decorated on one side with a scene of war; on the other side is a scene of hunting. Ceremonial knives such as this were used for circumcision.

definition of nature. Webster defines nature as "the essential character of something; inborn character or disposition." When the sin nature was removed, you were given the essential character of Christ.

There are two words that bring this exchange together: substitution and identification. Christ died a substitutionary death for us. In other words, He died in our place. When we place our faith in Christ, we are identified in Christ. We are given Christ's nature.

Look at the wording of verse 12. "Having been buried with Him in baptism, you were also raised with Him through faith." Paul was not referring to Christ's baptism at the Jordan; he was talking about what baptism symbolizes. Baptism tells the story of Christ's death, burial, and resurrection. When we are baptized, we go into the water symbolizing His death; we go under the water symbolizing His burial; we come out of the water symbolizing His resurrection. By identification, you died and were buried with Him in baptism. "Or are you unaware that all of us who were baptized into Christ Jesus were baptized into His death?" (Rom. 6:3). By identification, you have been raised with Him through faith.

Our new nature in Christ is the result of identification with Christ.

3. Your new nature came through life in Christ (Col. 2:13).

"And when you were dead in trespasses and in the uncircumcision of your flesh, He made you alive with Him and forgave us all our trespasses."

Apart from the work of Christ, a new nature would be impossible. Our former position in Adam rendered us spiritually dead and separated from God. Verse 13 reminds us that we were dead in trespasses, and Christ made us alive with Him. This concept is echoed in the Letter to the Ephesians. "And you were dead in your trespasses and sins… But God, who is rich in mercy, because of His great love that He had for us, made us alive with the Messiah even though we were dead in trespasses. You are saved by grace!" (Eph. 2:1,4-5).

Not only were they dead in their trespasses, but the Gentiles of Colossae were also dead in the uncircumcision of their flesh. For Jews, circumcision indicated that a person belonged to God's covenant people. For Gentiles, "the uncircumcision of your flesh," was a reminder that they were outside the covenants and promises of God. The same idea is found in Ephesians 2:12-13: "At that time you were without the Messiah, excluded from the citizenship of Israel, and foreigners to the covenants of the promise, without hope and without God in the world. But now in Christ Jesus, you who were far away have been brought near by the blood of the Messiah."

Jews and Gentiles were separated from God by trespasses and sin. However, all of that changed when we were forgiven of our trespasses. Notice the extent of your forgiveness. Jesus didn't forgive some of your sins; He forgave all your sins. You have been made alive by God, and this new life is rooted in Christ.

4. Your new nature came through forgiveness by Christ (Col. 2:14-15).

"He erased the certificate of debt, with its obligations, that was against us and opposed to us, and has taken it out of the way by nailing it to the cross. He disarmed the rulers and authorities and disgraced them publicly; He triumphed over them by Him."

Left: A mikvot from the second temple period just below southern steps in Jerusalem. New believers would have been baptized here on the Day of Pentecost.

These two verses contain one of the greatest promises in the Bible. Paul told the believers in Colossae that Jesus "erased the certificate of debt, with its obligations … by nailing it to the cross."

Certificate of debt literally means "something written with the hand." A debtor would write out a certificate of debt to acknowledge what he owed. In a spiritual sense, everyone owes God a sin debt because we broke His law. Verse 14 teaches us that Christ erased the certificate of debt. Why? Paul told us at the end of verse 13: He forgave us all our trespasses.

Our sins were nailed to the cross and in Christ we are completely forgiven. Your new nature in Christ was made possible by Christ's work on the cross.

WORD STUDY
"Erased" (2:14)

Normally, debts were cancelled in Paul's day simply by X-ing out the certificate of debt. This indicated that the certificate was no longer valid, but, unfortunately, the record of the debt was still clearly visible for anyone to read. This was not an adequate metaphor for describing the amazing forgiveness that Jesus provides sinners. So, parting with the conventions of his day, Paul insisted that rather than merely X-ing out the certificate of debt, God completely "erased" it.

People in the first-century Greco-Roman world were much better at erasing than modern people are. We use high-tech inks that bond with the fiber of paper and are virtually indelible. We can scrub and scrub a piece of paper with the best of erasers and yet we just can't remove all of the traces of ink. Things were different back then. The ancients used natural inks made of charcoal and gum or oil. These inks did not soak into the parchment, but sat right on the surface of the page. A writer could take a damp sponge and wash off the surface of the written page and soon it would be as fresh and clean as if it had never been written on before. He could also take a long sharp flat-bladed knife, specially designed for this purpose, and scrape the letters off of the page. The ink would flake off and turn to powder. With one deep gust of breath, he could blow the powderized ink away and the page would be as pure and clean.

Paul insisted that this is what God has done with the believer's spiritual certificate of debt. God took the believer's sin list and completely erased it. When the believer appears before God on Judgment Day

and He consults His great accounting book to determine what sins the believer committed and what punishment he deserves, the record will be totally blank. The debit page will be clean, white, and pure. No trace of sin will be recorded there. Those who repented of their sins and believed in Jesus Christ will be judged just as if they had never sinned at all. This is why Paul wrote earlier that Christ will "present you holy, faultless, and blameless before Him" (Col. 1:22). (CQ)

Above: A 1st century B.C. scribe's bronze ink pot and pen scabbard.

5. Your new nature is realized in the knowledge of Christ (Col. 3:9-10).

"Do not lie to one another, since you have put off the old self with its practices and have put on the new self. You are being renewed in knowledge according to the image of your Creator."

As a Christian, you have been spiritually circumcised (cut off from the sin nature). You are completely identified with Christ in His righteousness. Your new nature did not begin with you. You were dead. It began with Jesus because He made you alive. You have been forgiven. Your sins were not forgiven in part, but all your trespasses have been removed.

Therefore, "do not lie to one another" (v. 9). Stop telling people that Christ's work was not enough. Stop living as though your sin nature is still holding you back. You are free!

Your past is behind you. You have put off the old self with its practices. Christ is your future because you have put on the new self.

Do not put a question mark where God puts a period.

How do you learn to live according to your new nature in Christ? You are being "renewed in knowledge according to the image of your Creator" (v. 10). In other words, believe what God has done. Spend time meditating on the finished work of Christ. Immerse yourself in gospel truth. Do not put a question mark where God puts a period. You are free.

Stop for just a moment. Let the weight of these truths become personal to you. What would life look like for a person who is no longer enslaved to sin, who is identified with Christ, who has new life in Christ, and whose sins are forgiven and never remembered again? Every excuse for living in defeat is removed.

You were saved by grace through faith. Now, you are a saint who has been given the righteous nature of Christ. You have a new nature in Christ.

A CLOSER LOOK

"Put off ... put on" (3:9-10)

The verbs translated "put off" and "put on" in Colossians 3:9-10 were often used to describe the acts of removing one's garments and putting on a new suit of clothes. Oddly, many Christians grossly underestimate the radical transformation that occurred when they repented and believed and were united with Jesus in His death and resurrection. They seem to think that Christ merely added a new spiritual nature to their old spiritual nature so that two equal powers now reside in them struggling for control. This is not what Paul described. People do not put fresh, clean clothes on over old, dirty clothes. They remove the old clothes before they put on the new ones. In a similar way, the "new man" was not merely added to the "old man." The "new self" replaced the "old self." (CQ)

Personal Reflection

1. The sin nature has been removed. How does that truth impact your view of personal sin? What other Scriptures support this truth?

2. Colossians 3:10 speaks of being "renewed in knowledge according to the image of your Creator." How would you discover more about the image or nature of Christ? Make a simple plan for discovering more of who you are in Christ.

1. Bill Gillham, *Lifetime Guarantee* (Eugene, OR: Harvest House, 1993), 90.
2. Richard R. Melick, Jr. *Philippians, Colossians, Philemon*, vol. 32 in *The New American Commentary* (Nashville: Broadman Press, 1991), 295
3. D. Martyn Lloyd-Jones, *Romans: The New Man* (Grand Rapids: Zondervan, 1972), 65.

No Longer a Bachelor[1]

When men are not married, we call them bachelors. When a bachelor chooses a woman to be his wife, usually there is an engagement period. During that time the man is still a bachelor, but even then there are indications his life is about to change—radically. During the wedding the bachelor promises himself to the woman, and the pastor pronounces them husband and wife. In an instant his situation changed. He is no longer a bachelor, he is a husband.

In his vows he promised to be a husband, and he hoped he'd be a good one. Still, sometimes problems arise in the relationship. Some husbands never quite grasp the concept. They continue to live as if their own interests and needs are primary. Perhaps they continue going out with the guys. Perhaps they spend all their money on themselves. Some even run around with other women, disregarding their vows to purity and monogamy. People may react by saying, "Doesn't he know he has a wife?" "Doesn't he know he made promises?" "Doesn't he know he is no longer a bachelor?"

The last question targets the problem. Regardless of how the husband lives after his marriage, he is no longer a bachelor. The solution is to realize and accept who he really is, a husband, and get on with that part of his life. Further, the more he fails to act like a husband, the more frustrated he will become. Everywhere he goes and no matter what he does, he has a voice inside reminding him he is not keeping the commitment he made. In other words, a married man cannot act like a bachelor and be happy in it.

When individuals come to Christ, it is similar to a wedding. In a single moment, promises are made which affect those persons the rest of their lives. Once Christians are converted, they become new persons. No matter what they do or how they live, they will always be the new person. Continuing the analogy, when a Christian disobeys Christ, it's similar to the husband who continues to live like a bachelor. The relationship with Christ is affected when Christians live disobedient lives. Even though their hearts may be deeply committed to the things of God, they will not experience the joy of salvation and will carry guilt and frustration into every aspect of their lives. Failure to achieve victory over sin is the result of living inappropriately. Christians cannot say, "that was my old person."

The point is very simple. At the time of conversion you are changed. You are regenerated. You are responsible for your life and your relationship with Christ. You cannot blame failure on anyone else, including a bad nature. If all the proper ingredients are in place, in time you should mature and become a victorious Christian.

1. Adapted from Rick Melick, *Called to Be Holy* (Nashville: LifeWay Press, 2001), 67-68.

CHAPTER 5

You Are Free In Christ

COLOSSIANS 2:16-23

A re Christians really free? The first time I seriously questioned this freedom was August 27, 2004. As I shared earlier, the morning started like most others. I finished reading the Bible, and I started to pray. As I was praying for needs in my family, the needs of the church kept barraging my mind. I started praying for needs of the church, but personal concerns came to mind. I began praying over personal concerns, but goals and expectations and to-do lists kept swirling in my head. Every time I attempted to focus on one thing, my mind became clouded with dozens of different things.

Whenever my mind is overwhelmed, the only thing I know to do is write my thoughts out on paper. I began writing everything that I needed to do and I wrote down everything I needed to be. I wrote out every goal I was trying to accomplish.

Over the next 45 minutes, I wrote down 15 personal concerns, 26 family concerns, and 89 work related concerns. There were 130 identifiable issues pressing for my time and attention. For example, I was told that if I was going to be a good pastor, I needed to be a soul-winner, a visionary, a disciple maker, a reader, a lifelong student, a counselor, a theologian, a peacemaker, and gospel-driven. I needed to be more loving, more gracious, and more accessible. I needed to shepherd the community, plant churches, and do follow up with visitors. I needed to prepare insightful messages, be a man of prayer, and guard my family time. That's just 18 of the 89 things on the work list.

The problem was I could never do more than a couple of things effectively. When I tried to focus on prayer, it seemed like relationships would suffer. When I tried to be intentional about sharing the gospel, I didn't develop as many leaders. When I attempted to spend time with family, I felt guilty for saying no to church-related things.

I constantly felt like I was letting God down. On that morning, I had a moment of clarity. I cannot do it! There is no way I can fulfill every expectation. There's not enough time in the day to do everything that can be done. As soon as one project

is completed, three others take its place. I could not control or accomplish the 130 things spinning in my head at that moment.

No sooner did the thought come to mind than these words followed, "Therefore, if the Son sets you free, you really will be free" (John 8:36). Those words sat on me like a weight. Free? Really? I'm not free. I'm anything but free. I'm in bondage to responsibilities and expectations.

As I was trying to process John 8:36, a second passage came to mind. "Come to Me, all of you who are weary and burdened, and I will give you rest. All of you, take up My yoke and learn from Me, because I am gentle and humble in heart, and you will find rest for yourselves. For My yoke is easy and My burden is light" (Matt. 11:28-30).

The burden of being a Christian, a husband, a father, a pastor, a friend is not light. How can this statement be true?

In all my efforts to meet expectations and do something for God, I missed what God was asking of me. He simply said, "Come to Me." I didn't have 130 things to do that morning; I had one thing to do. I needed to be with Christ.

On that morning, God started a revolution in my heart. He began pulling me back from performance-based living, and He brought me into a life of freedom. He helped me to see that when we are with Christ, He lives His life through us. Everything God desires to do in and through our lives He will accomplish out of the overflow of our relationship with Him.

Everything God desires to do in and through our lives He will accomplish out of the overflow of our relationship with Him.

I've grown up in the church, and I've been a pastor for a number of years. I've seen the fatigue and frustration that performance-based living does to Christians. Through the years, I've realized that I'm not the only Christian who felt the weight of expectations. Millions of Christians who attend churches every week are confused and worn down by what they think God wants. They've been told that God died for them; it's their job to live for Him. It sounds good, but that's the very foundation of religion! Doing for God, performing for God, getting it all together for God is the heartbeat of every major world religion. Christianity is different. Jesus does not prescribe a list of actions to keep us right with God; He offers eternal life.

In John 17:3, Jesus defined eternal life: "This is eternal life: that they may know You, the only true God, and the One You have sent—Jesus Christ." Eternal life is to know God. Jesus offers a relationship. You have been freed from the law. You are freed from the expectations of others. You are free to simply enjoy God. And here's the crazy part. As you enjoy fellowship with Him, you become like Him.

Norman Douty wrote, "If I am to be like Him, then God in His grace must do it, and the sooner I come to recognize it the sooner I will be delivered from another form of bondage. ... Forget about trying to be like Him. Instead of letting that fill your mind and heart, let Him fill it. Just behold Him, look upon Him through the Word. Come to the Word for one purpose and that is to meet the Lord. Not to get your mind crammed full of things about the sacred Word, but come to it to meet the Lord. Make it to be a medium, not of biblical scholarship, but of fellowship with Christ."[1]

If you feel like you're constantly letting God down, I understand. If you feel like your Christian life has become a routine, this lesson is for you. If you feel like the weight of expectations is too much to bear, just keep reading. You've already learned that Christ is all you need. In this lesson, you will see that Christ is all you need to be free.

Let's walk through the specifics of our freedom in Christ. There are three great principles of freedom found in Colossians 2:16-23.

1. You are free from the demands of the law (Col. 2:16-17).

"Therefore, don't let anyone judge you in regard to food and drink or in the matter of a festival or a new moon or a Sabbath day. These are a shadow of what was to come; the substance is the Messiah."

Those who embraced Jewish legalism taught that faith in Christ was not enough for salvation and maturity. If a person wanted to be right with God, that individual also needed to keep the Jewish ceremonial law. The specific prohibitions mentioned in verse 16 were dietary laws from Leviticus 11. These specific laws were a part of the ceremonial law that marked Israel as God's distinct people.

In relation to these laws, Paul said, "Don't let anyone judge you." The reason they were not to be judged is because they were no longer under the old covenant; they were under the new covenant. Under the new covenant, the dietary laws no longer applied. Jesus taught this truth in Mark 7:14-19. Paul reminded believers of this truth in Romans 14:17. Peter's vision in Acts 10:9-16 highlighted this truth.

The laws related to festivals and sacrifices were also a part of the ceremonial law. Festivals were annual Jewish celebrations (for example, Passover, Pentecost, and the Feast of Tabernacles). Sacrifices were offered on new moons or the first day of the month (Num. 28:11-14). Paul reminded believers at Colossae that they should not let anyone judge them in these matters. Why? They were no longer under the law; they were under grace (Rom. 6:14, 7:6; Gal. 5:18).

Finally, Paul mentioned the Sabbath. Just like the other parts of ceremonial law, the specific rules and regulations connected to Sabbath observance no longer apply to New Testament believers. While Christians are commanded to worship God and assemble together for encouragement and community (Heb. 10:25; Acts 2:46), Christians are not commanded to observe the Sabbath regulations in a strict Jewish sense. In fact, the New Testament issues warnings about imposing Sabbath restrictions on grace-oriented believers (Acts 15; Gal. 4:10-11; Rom. 14:5).

Is there a problem with Old Testament law? Not a bit. The Old Testament law served God's purpose completely. The law reveals our sin. Paul said, "I would not have known sin if it were not for the law. For example, I would not have known what it is to covet if the law had not said, Do not covet" (Rom. 7:7). The law reveals sin, shows the holiness of God, shows our desperation for God, and even reveals underlying principles for godly living. However, there is still one more major purpose of the law.

Colossians 2:17 says, "These are a shadow of what was to come; the substance is the Messiah." God's goal in the law was not to make dietary restrictions, or festivals, or special days our object of worship. All of these laws pointed to Christ. They were the shadow; Christ is the substance. The law described what was required by God, and Jesus fulfilled the law (Matt. 5:17). Therefore, when we have Christ, we don't need the shadow to keep us right with God; we have the substance that makes us righteous before God.

A CLOSER LOOK

Jewish Legalism

The command in Colossians 2:16 provides one of the most important evidences for the identification of the false teaching that threatened the church in Colossae. Although various religious movements used special diets and observed festivals including the new moon, the Sabbath day was a distinctly Jewish observance. Thus the statement confirms that the Colossian heresy was influenced by Jewish legalism. The false teachers were judging the Colossian Christians based on whether they fulfilled the dietary laws of the Old Testament (Lev. 7:22-27; 11:1-23; 17:10-16; Deut. 14:3-21), kept the Jewish ritual calendar (Lev. 23; Deut. 16:1-17) including the New Moon celebration (Num. 10:10; 28:11-15; Neh. 10:33; Ps. 81:3; Isa. 66:23; Ezek. 46:6), or observed the Sabbath regulation that prohibited any work on the last day of the week (Ex. 20:8-11; 23:12; 31:12-17; 35:1-3; Lev. 23:3; Deut. 5:12-15). (CQ)

Brownie Points

"Brownie points" is a cultural expression used to describe what a person earns by doing good deeds or favors, usually for someone who is in authority over them. There are several suggestions on where the expression came from:

(1) Girl Scouts or "Brownies" earned merit badges through doing good deeds and thus the expression came into existence.

(2) George R. Brown, a railroad superintendent, who developed a system of incentives for employees who coined the phrase to describe the merits and rewards earned in Brown's system.

(3) Curtis Publishing Company offered "brownies" or stamps to be exchanged for goods to young people who delivered their magazines.

Regardless of how the word came into existence, the concept exists in many people's minds. Some apply it to a relationship with God, in which they do good deeds and God grants them favors in return.

What are some of the acts that people believe they must do in order to get God's so-called brownie points?

How do you think God sees this approach?

The idea that the law is the shadow and Christ is the substance is echoed in the Letter to the Galatians. "The law, then, was our guardian until Christ, so that we could be justified by faith" (Gal. 3:24). Notice the word *until*. Paul didn't say, "The law was our guardian with Christ." That would suggest that the law is protecting

us from God's wrath while being in Christ. We know that is not the case. No one is justified by works; we are justified by faith (2:16; 3:24). In Galatians, Paul told believers that the law was our guardian and Christ is our righteousness. In Colossians, Paul told believers that the law was the shadow and Christ is the substance. Both are saying the same thing.

When you have Christ, you are free from the legalistic demands of the law. Christ is all you need.

Shadow (2:17)

The Old Testament sacrificial system anticipated Jesus' death as the supreme and effective sacrifice (Heb. 9:11-14; 10:1-10). The Sabbath rest pictured that believers had given up their efforts to work their way to God by their attempts to keep the law and now rested in His grace alone (Heb. 4:9-10). (CQ)

2. You are free from the religious games of others (Col. 2:18-19).

"Let no one disqualify you, insisting on ascetic practices and the worship of angels, claiming access to a visionary realm and inflated without cause by his unspiritual mind. He doesn't hold on to the head, from whom the whole body, nourished and held together by its ligaments and tendons, develops with growth from God."

Maybe you've heard some of the following statements. "I know what the Bible says about this subject, but God showed me a new truth." "God gave me a vision for you. He told me that if you would just do these four things, you too would go to a new level with God." "If you just had _____ as a spiritual gift, God could do more with you."

The possibilities for religious games are endless. Religious games thrive when theology is missing. They are attempts to add something to Christ for deeper meaning, greater knowledge, and a better experience. While the options are endless, they essentially say, "If you knew what I knew or had what I had—then you would really experience God."

These teachings were at the core of gnosticism and mysticism. They are based in the belief that truth is determined individually and internally. If so, the possibilities for error are endless.

Paul said, "Let no one disqualify you." This is also translated, "Let no one keep defrauding you." Don't let anyone move you away from truth or keep you back from the reality of Christ. Deep union with God is not made through mystical connections; it is secured by Christ and experienced as we abide in Him. Christ is all you need.

WORD STUDY

"Disqualify" (2:18)

The verb "disqualify" referred to an umpire who disqualified a contestant for failing to keep the rules. Paul's point was that the Colossians should not allow the false teachers to serve as their spiritual umpires as if they bore the authority to kick them off the playing field for failing to live up to the umpire's rules. The warning thus echoes that in 2:16: "Don't let anyone judge you." (CQ)

These false teachers possibly were engaged in the worship of angels. The Bible clearly addresses whom we are to worship. Jesus told Satan, "Worship the Lord your God, and serve only Him" (Matt. 4:10). Humans are not alone in our worship of God. According to Isaiah 6:1-4 and Revelation 5:11-12, the angels themselves worship God. Why would we worship angels if they too are called to worship God? You don't need another object to worship. Christ is all you need.

Left: Mandaic ("Syriac Script") Incantation Bowl. The angel Gabriel and various idols and spirits are invoked to protect Chosroes, son of Apra-Hormiz, and his family.

The false teachers were also "claiming access to a visionary realm." It's scary to think of how many religions, cults, and schisms have been started with the phrase, "I had a vision." It is not that God has been unwilling to reveal Himself; the problem is that people do not like what He has revealed. Therefore, they indulge an "unspiritual mind." They chase after new experiences instead of holding "on to the head, from whom the whole body, nourished and held together by its ligaments and tendons, develops with growth from God" (2:19). Who is the head? Christ! Christ is all you need.

The answer to spiritual depth and growth is not a new teaching, a new revelation, or a new gift or power. The answer to spiritual growth is to "hold on to the head." Don't let anyone persuade you that Christ is not enough for spiritual growth. If Christ is not all you need, then Christ is not what you need.

You are free from the religious games of others.

The answer to spiritual growth is to "hold on to the head."

---

3. You are free from the ascetic expectations of the world (Col. 2:20-23).

"If you died with the Messiah to the elemental forces of this world, why do you live as if you still belonged to the world? Why do you submit to regulations: 'Don't handle, don't taste, don't touch'? All these regulations refer to what is destroyed by being used up; they are commands and doctrines of men. Although these have a reputation of wisdom by promoting ascetic practices, humility, and severe treatment of the body, they are not of any value in curbing self-indulgence."

Many of the world's religions emphasize ascetic practices for spiritual growth. These practices involve some form of self-denial. People are encouraged to take a vow of poverty or celibacy, fast for a month, pray five times a day, abstain from certain pleasures, or endure certain pain.

WORD STUDY

"Ascetic practices" (2:23)

The word translated "ascetic practices" is a compound of the word translated "worship" in Colossians 2:18. It adds to the word *worship* a prefix that often means "pretended" or "so-called." The term probably implies that the worship of God the mystics experienced during their visions was a figment of their own imagination. Ironically, the mystics claimed that their practices were characterized by deep humility, but this humility also was a pretended one. Paul had already charged that the mystics' practices puffed them up and made them arrogant (Col. 2:18). (CQ)

Asceticism is popular because it is a common belief that righteousness is gained through self-denial. Many Christians are pulled into this belief because there is an element of truth in that statement. In Matthew 16:24, Jesus told His disciples, "If anyone wants to come with Me, he must deny himself, take up his cross, and follow Me." Part of following Christ is denying self. However, the difference is in the purpose of self-denial.

Religion emphasizes self-denial as a means to make one right with the divine. It shows contrition and sincerity. You do these things to gain a better standing. In essence, your self-denial earns God's approval. Christianity teaches just the opposite. Nothing we could do would ever make us right with God. Isaiah 64:6 reminds us, "All of us have become like something unclean, and all our righteous acts are like a polluted garment." Our best is not good enough. Our discipline, our sacrifices, and our good intentions are not sufficient to reconcile us to God.

However, Christ did what we could never do. He lived a sinless life, He died a substitutionary death, He rose from the dead in victorious life, and He offers eternal life to those who will repent by placing faith in Him. When Jesus calls us to deny self, it is not for the purpose of making us right with God. He already did that on the cross. By denying self, Christ lives through us.

By denying self, Christ lives through us.

We don't need man-made rules to promote spirituality. We have Christ. Sure, man-made restrictions have "a reputation of wisdom." However, they do not have any value in curbing self-indulgence. Asceticism may seem spiritual, but it actually feeds and gratifies the flesh.

God is not asking you to submit to the ascetic rules of the world. You are free to enjoy Him. Let that idea sink in. You are free in Christ.

Personal Reflection

1. Think through your life as a Christian. What expectations are you trying to fulfill? Make a list of the personal, biblical and/or religious expectations that come to mind. (Examples: I'm supposed to pray daily. I need to read my Bible daily. I need to go to church each week.)

2. Based on the list you just made, are you living as someone who is free? According to Paul, what does it look like to be free? In addition to Colossians 2, read Galatians 5:1,13-14, Philippians 3, and Romans 6:17-23, 8:12-17.

A CLOSER LOOK

Are Christians still under parts of the Mosaic Law?

The concern usually goes like this: "God gave us the entire Bible. Is it wrong to teach people to obey the Ten Commandments? I know that we are free from certain parts of the law, but shouldn't we still obey others?"

These are great questions. As Christians, we know the entire Bible is inspired by God and is "profitable for teaching, for rebuking, for correcting, for training in righteousness" (2 Tim. 3:16). We also know that being free from the law does not give us a license to break God's commands and to steal, murder, or engage in idol worship (Rom. 6:15-16).

So are Christians still under parts of the Mosaic Law? Let's allow Scripture to clearly address this question.

- "For sin will not rule over you, because you are not under law but under grace" (Rom. 6:14).
- "Therefore, my brothers, you also were put to death in relation to the law through the crucified body of the Messiah" (Rom. 7:4).
- "But if you are led by the Spirit, you are not under the law" (Gal. 5:18).
- "But now we have been released from the law, since we have died to what held us, so that we may serve in the new way of the Spirit and not in the old letter of the law" (Rom. 7:6).

God's Word is clear. Christians are no longer under the law. You are free in Christ. However, that truth does not mean Old Testament law is irrelevant. The law serves a very real and ongoing purpose. The law reveals the holiness of God and personal sin. The law reveals the depravity of sinners and our inability to make ourselves right with God. The law was our tutor who led us to Christ.

In actuality, law and grace work hand in hand. The law reveals sin and shows our need for a Savior. Grace conquers sin and offers us eternal life. We need the law to point us to Christ; we need grace to reconcile us to Christ.

God does not ask us to follow Old Testament commands to be right with Him. Jesus' sacrificial work and bodily resurrection has made us right before God. However, by understanding the law, the ceremonies, the sacrifices, and the underlying principles—it deepens our understanding of who Christ is, what He has done for us, and how God wants us to live.

1. Miles J. Stanford, *The Complete Green Letters* (Grand Rapids: Zondervan, 1983), 16.

CHAPTER 6

You Are Positioned In Christ

COLOSSIANS 3:1-4

Awhile back, we were having a family discussion about hard work and the types of jobs available to young people today. My daughters were 8 and 9 years old at the time. Between you and me, I don't think that it's ever too early to instill a solid work ethic in our kids. At any rate, my wife was reminiscing over her former places of employment and sharing stories about various positions. After a few stories, my oldest daughter asked, "Dad, how many jobs have you had in your life?"

The question took me by surprise. I don't think I've ever counted. I said, "Well, my first real job was at a Christian school when I was 14. I cleaned classrooms, hallways, and the cafeteria after school. I was paid $2.55 an hour." My girls' eyes got as big as saucers. Even at 8 and 9, they knew that was not a lot of money. "Then I worked at a yogurt store, then a major retail store, then at a clothing store in the mall. In college, I worked security at night for one year. I managed a gym for the next two years. During summer breaks, I worked on a survey crew. Each December, I worked retail through the winter break. Then there was a small stint waiting tables, three years as a store manager at another retail store, a year with a shipping company," and the list just kept going.

I was a bit startled. Since the age of 14, I've had 18 different jobs. When I say it out loud, it sounds like I have difficulty keeping a job. To spin it in a positive light, I prefer to think that I was covering my bases and discovering my natural talents. Regardless of what I call it, there have been a lot of jobs.

Based on that experience, I feel qualified to make the next statement. Our position determines our function and benefits. When my position was cleaning up after school, both my function and my benefits were less than glamorous. When my position was managing a gym, my function shifted from doer to overseer. My benefits increased slightly due to more responsibility. While serving in the position of a lead pastor, my function is to equip and encourage believers, oversee the ministry, and lead based on vision. As you might imagine, the benefits of that position are better. Our position determines our function and benefits.

Our position determines our function and benefits.

Take that concept and transfer it to your spiritual life. The Bible says a lot about our spiritual position. Prior to Christ, we were positioned in Adam. In Adam, people are "dead in trespasses and sins," because "in Adam all die" (Eph. 2:1; 1 Cor. 15:22). Our function as sinners placed us at odds with God. We walked "according to the ways of this world" (Eph. 2:2). There were no benefits with that position because we were dead to God and alive to sin. We were "without the Messiah, excluded from the citizenship of Israel, and foreigners to the covenants of the promise, without hope and without God in the world" (Eph. 2:12). However, when a person enters into a relationship with Christ, everything changes.

Our position changes from being in Adam to being in Christ. Paul described this new position with the phrases, "in Christ," "in Him," or "in the Beloved" (Phil. 1:1; Eph. 1:6-7). As our position changed, so did our function and benefits. We went from "children of wrath" to those with the "ministry of reconciliation (Eph. 2:3; 2 Cor. 5:18). At one point, we were enemies of God, but now we are worshipers of God (Rom. 5:10; John 4:24). As our function changed, so did our benefits. We have transitioned from spiritual poverty to spiritual wealth. God "has blessed us in Christ with every spiritual blessing in the heavens" (Eph. 1:3). We have gone from sinners to saints, from separated to reconciled, from death to life, from broken to complete. All of this change happens as a result of our new position in Christ.

What if the key to spiritual breakthrough is a better understanding of your position in Christ?

Our position determines our function and benefits. How well do you know your new position in Christ? Is it possible that you're functioning from your old position in Adam?

Are you aware of the benefits available to you in Christ? What if the key to spiritual breakthrough is a better understanding of your position in Christ?

A CLOSER LOOK
Our Position in Christ

Since the believer's "life is hidden with the Messiah in God" (Col. 3:3), the believer's spiritual position is where Christ is, "seated at the right hand of God" (v. 1) Heaven is "where Christ is." Christ is present in heaven, not as a mere worshiper who bows before the Father's feet, but as a reigning King who is enthroned at the Father's right hand. The position at the Father's right hand is a position of authority and supremacy. As the One seated at the Father's right hand, Jesus is "head over every ruler and authority" (Col. 2:10) and reigning conqueror of all His enemies including sin, death, Satan, and his demons (Eph. 1:20-23; 2:6). Believers need to reflect on their new identity as those who are united with Christ and thus reign with Christ. (CQ)

In this chapter, we are going to explore the basics of our position in Christ. The primary text will be Colossians 3:1-4.

So if you have been raised with the Messiah, seek what is above, where the Messiah is, seated at the right hand of God. Set your minds on what is above, not on what is on the earth. For you have died, and your life is hidden with the Messiah in God. When the Messiah, who is your life, is revealed, then you also will be revealed with Him in glory.

There are three parts of positional truth covered in these verses. Each part impacts a different aspect of your life in Christ. Let's work through each truth.

1. Our position in Christ impacts our pursuits (Col. 3:1).

"So if you have been raised with the Messiah, seek what is above, where the Messiah is, seated at the right hand of God."

When I refer to pursuits, I'm talking about the things that drive us. It could be good pursuits like God, His kingdom, loving people, or serving others. It could be neutral pursuits like education, relaxation, or hobbies. It could also be harmful pursuits like drugs, sinful relationships, or greed. We all have pursuits. However, our position in Christ impacts those pursuits.

What does this mean: "So if you have been raised with the Messiah"? This phrase is understood in light of the truths from preceding chapters. These truths include our new nature in Christ, identification with Christ, and His substitutionary death. We covered each of those truths in chapter 4. Here's a quick review.

When we are saved, we are given a new nature in Christ. The sin nature is removed, and Christ's nature is received (2 Cor. 5:17). Prior to salvation, we were positioned in Adam; after salvation, we are positioned in Christ.

Just as our old nature came through identification with Adam, our new nature comes through identification with Christ. By placing faith in Christ (and His finished work on the cross), we identify with His story. His death on the cross becomes our death to sin. His resurrection from the dead becomes our resurrection to life. Romans 6:3-4 and Colossians 2:12 clearly teach this principle. Our identity is in Him (Col. 3:4).

His death on the cross becomes our death to sin. His resurrection from the dead becomes our resurrection to life.

This new identity in Christ is the result of His substitutionary death. Jesus did not deserve death; Jesus never sinned (2 Cor. 5:21; Heb. 4:15). Instead, He willingly endured the cross to pay the penalty for our sin (Heb. 12:2). He died in our place as our substitute.

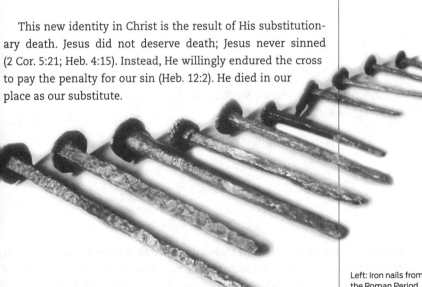

Left: Iron nails from the Roman Period

As the pieces come together, we see the bigger picture of redemption. We have a new nature because of Christ. We have a new position because of Christ. We have a new life because of Christ. We have a new story because of Christ. We have a new identity because of Christ. Is it any wonder that Paul said, "I have been crucified with Christ and I no longer live, but Christ lives in me" (Gal. 2:19b-20a)? Spiritually speaking, we died and our new life is found in Christ.

With those truths as our foundation, notice the connection between Colossians 2:20 and Colossians 3:1. "If you died with the Messiah (2:20) … if you have been raised with the Messiah" (3:1). Do you see the connection? In Colossians 2:20, Paul was saying, *If you died with the Messiah, then you are dead to the following things.* In Colossians 3:1, Paul was saying, *If you have been raised with the Messiah, then you are alive to the following things.* The statements are two sides on the same coin of redemption.

LEARNING ACTIVITY
Two Sides of the Coin of Redemption

"If you died with the Messiah" (Col. 2:20)
To what things have you died?

"If you have been raised with the Messiah" (Col. 3:1)
To what things are you now alive?

As a result of being raised with the Messiah, we are alive to new pursuits. When we were dead in our sin nature, we were unable to pursue the things of God. Ephesians 2:1-3 gives us a perfect description of what we pursued prior to Christ.

And you were dead in your trespasses and sins in which you previously walked according to the ways of this world, according to the ruler who exercises authority over the lower heavens, the spirit now working in the disobedient. We too all previously lived among them in our fleshly desires, carrying out the inclinations of our flesh and thoughts, and we were by nature children under wrath as the others were also.

We were dead in our trespasses and sins. We walked according to the ways of the world. We lived by the dictates of another ruler. We acted on our fleshly desires. We indulged our sinful thoughts. We were by nature children of wrath. These were our pursuits. We were not chasing God; we were pursuing sin at every level.

However, since we "have died with the Messiah" (2:20) and "have been raised up with the Messiah" (3:1)—we are able to pursue other things. Instead of seeking sinful pleasures, we are to "keep seeking the things above." The phrase "keep seeking" is in the present tense indicating continuous action. We are to continuously seek the things above.

What are the things above? "Things above" refers to God, His kingdom activity, and His interactions with us. It will include God's plans and purposes. It incorporates the realities of heaven, our position in Christ, our possessions in Christ, and Christ Himself. We are to pursue these things with our lives.

While God wants us to enjoy family, friends, leisure time, and hobbies, they cannot become our primary pursuits. These things can make life enjoyable, but they cannot become our life. Our position in Christ impacts our pursuits.

2. Our position in Christ directs our mind (Col. 3:2).

"Set your minds on what is above, not on what is on the earth."

It has been said that every Christian is engaged in a battle for the mind. Whoever controls the mind controls the person. Spiritually speaking, Christians have already obtained the victory in Christ. Death, hell, and the grave have been defeated. We are no longer slaves of sin; we are slaves of righteousness (Rom. 6:18). And while victory describes our spiritual reality, defeat often describes our mental outlook.

While victory describes our spiritual reality, defeat often describes our mental outlook.

If we do not believe we are free, if we do not think in terms of victory, if we do not see ourselves as God sees us—we will live in spiritual defeat. We will ask God for resources that we already possess. We will pray for help that is already ours. We will wait on answers He has already given.

Once a person enters a relationship with Christ, the greatest hindrance to victory is not the power of sin but the mindset of Adam. It is for that reason that Paul challenged believers to "be transformed by the renewing of your mind" (Rom. 12:2), to "be renewed in the spirit of your minds" (Eph. 4:23), to take "every thought captive to obey Christ" (2 Cor. 10:5). Whoever controls the mind controls the person.

Colossians 3:2 addresses the mindset that flows from our position in Christ. "Set your minds on what is above, not on what is on the earth." Go back to my earlier statement. Our position determines our function and benefits. This statement is about our function. How do we function in this new position? First, we are to pursue the things above. We saw that in the last point. Second, we are to set our minds on the things above. Third, we are not to set our minds on the things of the earth.

What does it practically look like to set our minds on things above? Here are just a few ways to apply that truth.

- Spend time in God's Word.
- Communicate with God in prayer.
- Reflect upon your identity in Christ. (Refer to the list provided at the end of chapter 2.)
- Meditate on Christ's life, His mission, and His nature.
- Consider your possessions in Christ (Eph. 1:3-14).
- Make it a priority to pursue His Kingdom and His righteousness.
- Focus on the eternal instead of the temporal.
- Think about "whatever is true, whatever is honorable, whatever is just, whatever is pure, whatever is lovely, whatever is commendable—if there is any moral excellence and if there is any praise—dwell on these things" (Phil. 4:8).
- Remember your position in Christ.

What does it look like to set your mind on the things of the earth? Here are a few common examples.

- Fill your mind with newspapers, magazines, and books.
- Spend every evening watching TV or movies.
- Focus solely on the here and now (and not on eternity).
- Allow undisciplined thoughts to linger and flourish in your mind.
- Cram work into every waking moment.
- Develop more of a passion for sports than for Christ.
- Build up wealth in this life without any regards to eternity.
- Fill your schedule with ball practices, dance recitals, affinity groups, vacations, church activities, hobbies, etc.

Before you get too upset with that last list, I want to encourage you to view both lists through our freedom in Christ. To accept everything from the first list and reject everything on the second list will only lead to legalism and bondage. Many of the items from the second list are good activities. There is nothing wrong with ball practices, dance recitals, church activities, hobbies, sports, newspapers, books, etc. The question is not, "Are these things sinful?" The question is, "Do they interfere with setting our minds on things above?"

Good things, without moderation, can become big problems. If other pursuits do not allow us time to spend with God, or reflect on the ideas of Philippians 4:8, or pursue His Kingdom—then we may need to back way from some good activities.

God wants us to enjoy life. Jesus promised that He came to give life (John 10:10). However, God knows that our greatest joy is not found apart from Him but with Him. Our position in Him will direct our mind.

Good things, without moderation, can become big problems.

A CLOSER LOOK
"What is on the earth" (3:2)

Although Paul condemned materialism elsewhere (1 Tim. 6:1-10), his concern in Colossians 3:2 is different. No evidence suggests that the false teachers were obsessed with land, houses, and other possessions. However, their ritualism did make them overly concerned with the foods they ate, the beverages they consumed, and the objects that they touched. Their rigorous efforts to keep Jewish dietary laws and to honor taboos related to contact with unclean objects prompted obsession with earthly rather than heavenly things. This did not reflect the heavenly perspective that those who resurrected and ascended with Christ should possess. Furthermore, the phrase translated "what is on the earth" appears again in Colossians 3:5 ("what belongs to your worldly nature") in which it refers to sins such as "sexual immorality, impurity, lust, evil desire, and greed, which is idolatry." (CQ)

3. Our position in Christ reveals our true life (Col. 3:3-4).

"For you have died, and your life is hidden with the Messiah in God. When the Messiah, who is your life, is revealed, then you also will be revealed with Him in glory."

How would you describe your life? Many people respond with a mixture of facts. They would give their age, marital status, choice of careers, alma mater, number of kids, where they live, personal hobbies, and so forth. And while all of those things describe your life from a temporal perspective, they do not describe your life from an eternal perspective. Paul said, "For you have died (your old nature), and your (new) life is hidden with the Messiah in God."

Your real life, the essence of who you are, is defined by your new identity in Christ. You died to the old nature. You died to sin (Rom. 6:11). You died to this world's system (Gal. 6:14). Your new life is not of this world; your new life is hidden with the Messiah in God.

Your real life, the essence of who you are, is defined by your new identity in Christ.

When Paul described our new life as "hidden with Christ in God," he was talking about oneness with Christ. Our position is "in Christ, in Him, or in the Beloved"

Left: The meat market or "Macellum" at Puteoli, Italy. Under the new covenant, the dietary laws no longer applied.

(Phil. 1:1; Eph. 2:6-7). We are in Him; that speaks of oneness. However, Jesus promised that the Father would send another Helper who "remains with you and will be in you" (John 14:17). This Helper is identified as the Holy Spirit. While we are in Him (Christ), His Spirit is in us (Rom. 8:11). No Christian has a personal standing apart from Christ. We are either "hidden with Christ in God" or we are "without the Messiah ... without hope and without God in the world" (Eph. 2:12).

Our lives are so hidden with Messiah in God that we share His Spirit (1 Cor. 6:17), His divine nature (2 Pet. 1:4), His glory through suffering (Rom. 8:17), and even His inheritance (Col. 1:12). Our lives are truly hidden with Messiah in God.

Colossians 3:4 says, "When the Messiah, who is your life, is revealed, then you also will be revealed with Him in glory." Jesus is not a part of your life; He is your life.

Jesus is not a part of your life; He is your life.

The further we walk with God, the more we see "self" disappear. As new believers, our mindset is often "Me and God." We live from the perspective that God is a great addition to us. After walking with Christ for a while, our mindset shifts to "God and me." We see the importance of God remaining first in our lives. Once we understand positional truth, our language soon becomes "God." He is our life. "I no longer live, but Christ lives in me" (Gal. 2:20).

LEARNING ACTIVITY

The Journey of Our Walk with God

Infancy stage: "Me and God"

Focus:

Pitfalls and Dangers:

Developing stage: "God and me"

Focus:

Pitfalls and Dangers:

Mature stage: "God"

Focus:

Pitfalls and Dangers:

Colossians 3:4 tells us that there will be a time when both Christ and His followers will be revealed. "When the Messiah ... is revealed, then you also will be revealed with Him in glory." John describes that scene in Revelation 19:11-14,16.

> Then I saw heaven opened, and there was a white horse. Its rider is called Faithful and True, and He judges and makes war in righteousness. His eyes were like a fiery flame, and many crowns were on His head. He had a name written that no one knows except Himself. He wore a robe stained with blood, and His name is the Word of God. The armies that were in heaven followed Him on white horses, wearing pure white linen. ... And He has a name written on His robe and on His thigh: KING OF KINGS AND LORD OF LORDS.

There will be a day when what has been hidden will be revealed. On that day, our Savior will return, not as a suffering servant, but as a reigning King.

Your position in Christ reveals your true life. Your spiritual reality in Christ is just as real as your physical reality in this world. In some ways, it is more real. There will be a day when your physical reality will vanish. Dust will return to dust. The spiritual reality of who you are in Christ will never vanish. Our position in Christ reveals our true life. You are who God says you are.

Personal Reflection

1. You can pinpoint positional truths by the phrases "in Him" and "in Christ." Looking through Colossians, what are some other positional verses in this book?

2. When a couple gets married, there is a positional change. They go from single to married. Possessions shift from "mine" to "ours." Two paths now converge into one. Scripture tells us that Christ is the Bridegroom; the church is the Bride. What positional changes can you see from this union?

A CLOSER LOOK

Christianity is about Christ

We began this study by saying, "Christ is all you need." That phrase summarizes Paul's overall theme. I also shared that Colossians is the most Christ-centered book in the Bible. Did you notice how this entire section (3:1-4) is focused on Christ? Paul used the phrases "with the Messiah" (3:1), "where the Messiah is" (3:1), "with the Messiah" (3:3), "when the Messiah" (3:4), and "with Him" (3:4). At each point, he stressed the sufficiency and completeness of Christ (2:10).

Unfortunately, many Christians still fail to pursue Christ as their life. He is not a great addition to our life; He is our life. Your position in Christ is the basis for your entire Christian life. Contrary to popular belief, "Me and God" do not make a great team. "Me" tends to get in the way of "God." Let Him be your life. Colossians helps us see the rally cry of the Reformers. Christianity is about Christ, Christ always, and Christ alone.

CHAPTER 7

You Are Empowered Through Christ

COLOSSIANS 1:5b-6,11,27,29; 3:5—4:6

I n less than six months, I'll turn 40 years old. I know 40 is a dreaded year for a lot of people, but I'm trying to look on the bright side. It's better than not turning 40!

In those 40 years, I've been blessed to marry my sweetheart, start a family, achieve educational goals, travel the world, plant multiple churches, invest my life in God's kingdom, and eat a lot of BBQ. I have no complaints. I do have several concerns.

The closer I've crept towards 40, the more I've noticed that some things have stopped working, some things hurt while working, and some things work differently than they've worked in the past. For example, the hair on top of my head stopped working, but the hair in my ears puts in overtime. My arms are suddenly not long enough to read a book. Who knew that "monkey arms" were a good thing? My joints either freeze in silence or they pop with loud disapproval. Finally, I'm convinced that my metabolism stopped working about seven years ago. Gaining weight while eating salads will make you long for the metabolism of your youth.

For those 55 and older, you're probably thinking, "Just wait! You haven't seen anything yet." For those 25 and younger, you're probably thinking, "It will never happen to me." Perspective is a funny thing isn't it?

With all of the changes my body has gone through, the most apparent has been a lack of strength in the gym. I've worked out four to five times a week since the age of 13. I've always been in decent shape, and I've always had plenty of strength to accomplish my goals. But things have changed. There's more weight coming off the barbell than going on.

After struggling to keep up, I finally decided to get some help. I researched nutritional supplements, muscle building products, and natural remedies for strength. I narrowed things down to a few key supplements, and I started a supplement routine. After taking the supplements for several weeks, I noticed a difference. While I don't feel 18 again, I at least feel like my mid 30's. I'll take it!

Here's my point. Strength fades. There will come a time in everyone's life when the strength we possess is not sufficient for the challenge we're facing. It could be a lack of physical strength, or spiritual strength, or emotional strength. The longer we live, the more we see the wisdom (and necessity) in drawing strength from another source.

One of the greatest passages that describes finding strength in weakness is found in 2 Corinthians 12:9-10. Paul prayed that God would remove his thorn in the flesh. Instead of removing the thorn, God shared an incredible truth in verse 9. "My grace is sufficient for you, for power is perfected in weakness." Paul's response is found in verse 10. "Therefore, I will most gladly boast all the more about my weaknesses, so that Christ's power may reside in me. So I take pleasure in weaknesses, insults, catastrophes, persecutions, and in pressures, because of Christ. For when I am weak, then I am strong."

Paul made an incredible discovery. He found that his strength was not enough, and Christ's strength was sufficient. Paul discovered pleasure in weakness because his weakness became an outlet for God's strength.

How does that happen? How do we go from struggling under the weight of the problem to taking pleasure in our weakness? It's one thing to quote Philippians 4:13; it's another thing to live 2 Corinthians 12:9.

In our final chapter, we're going to discover how our life is empowered by Christ. You will see the connection between your weakness and Christ's strength. You will find specific ways that Christ desires to live His strength through you. We may not be strong enough to handle every challenge, but His strength is enough. His grace is sufficient. His power is perfected in weakness. Christ is all we need.

His strength is enough. His grace is sufficient. His power is perfected in weakness.

1. You are empowered to bear spiritual fruit through Christ (Col. 1:5b-6).

"You have already heard about this hope in the message of truth, the gospel that has come to you. It is bearing fruit and growing all over the world, just as it has among you since the day you heard it and recognized God's grace in the truth."

The placement of these verses is key to applying the truth. In the prison epistles (Colossians, Ephesians, Philippians, and Philemon), Paul's format is very similar. He starts with what we should know, and he moves to what we should do. Colossians 1–2 spells out proper belief; Colossians 3–4 encourages proper behavior. Before we can live in truth, we must first understand truth.

In 1:6, Paul declared the truth of the gospel. The truth is that the gospel "has come to you," and "it is bearing fruit and growing all over the world, just as it has among you…" The gospel is bearing fruit.

What is the gospel? The gospel is the good news that Jesus died for sinners, He was raised from the dead, and He offers eternal life to those who will repent by placing faith in Jesus Christ. As a result of what Christ has done, people can experience a reconciled relationship with God. That's good news!

The gospel accomplishes the work God intends. In verse 6 Paul wrote that the gospel was bearing fruit and spreading not only to the Colossians in the Lycus valley, but all over the world.

There is a second aspect to bearing fruit that is also mentioned. The gospel is not just bearing fruit *around* you; it is also bearing fruit *in* you. Bearing fruit is when God manifests His character in you and/or lives His purposes through you.

Bearing fruit is when God manifests His character in you and/or lives His purposes through you.

A CLOSER LOOK

Bearing fruit and growing

The agricultural metaphors "bearing fruit and growing" in 1:6 recalled Jesus' teaching in the parable of the sower (Mark 4:1-9, 13-20) and the parable of the growing seed (Mark 4:26-29). Mark, the writer who recorded these two parables, was with Paul when this letter was written (Col. 4:10). The instructions at the close of the Epistle show that Mark had plans to travel to Colossae, perhaps to share the stories of Jesus from his Gospel with the Colossians. The allusions to Jesus' parables stress God's power to work through the gospel to change people's lives and to produce in them an abundant harvest of righteousness. (CQ)

How does the gospel of Christ lead to fruitful lives? John 15:4-5 gives the answer.

> Remain in Me, and I in you. Just as a branch is unable to produce fruit by itself unless it remains on the vine, so neither can you unless you remain in Me. I am the vine; you are the branches. The one who remains in Me and I in him produces much fruit, because you can do nothing without Me.

We do not have the power to produce spiritual fruit in ourselves. Anyone who has ever tried to break an addiction, or overcome secret sin, or obey all the commands of the Bible can testify. We can manage sin for a season, but we cannot produce spiritual fruit. In Christ, we are empowered to bear fruit. As we abide in Him, He bears fruit through us.

2. You are empowered for challenges through Christ (Col. 1:11).

"May you be strengthened with all power, according to His glorious might, for all endurance and patience, with joy."

The Greek word translated "strengthened" in verse 11 signifies continuous action. God continues to strengthen us. He doesn't just give strength for this trial, and that problem, and those circumstances. He continually strengthens us with all power, according to His glorious might.

Notice the measurement for strength. God does not restore you to the height of your strength. He does not give you the strength of the strongest person you know. Instead, He strengthens you according to His glorious might. Since His power is unlimited, your strength is never exhausted.

Since His power is unlimited, your strength is never exhausted.

That's good news! When people experience the death of a loved one, job loss, divorce, major illness, financial ruin, or any number of other tragic circumstances, their prayer is often the same. "God, I don't think I can do this. I don't have the strength. I'm worn out. I was hurting before this happened. What do I do?"

Verse 11 is God's reply. As a Christian, you will never face a challenge alone. Christ is with you and in you. His strength is unlimited, and He will continue to strengthen you according to His glorious might.

A CLOSER LOOK
Empowered

The grammar of the original text and context of verse 11 make it clear that God empowers the believer to walk worthy of Him (see 1:10). The believer simply cannot do this by his own strength. "All power" and "glorious might" remind readers that God's power is unlimited. He is more than capable of granting every resource necessary for godly living. In particular, God's power grants believers strength to endure. Our energy would quickly deplete and our resources would soon fizzle out, if God did not sustain us. His power enables believers to "remain grounded and steadfast in the faith" and "not shifted away from the hope of the gospel" (Col. 1:23). (CQ)

Two other words help us see the scope of God's strength. The word *endurance* refers to being patient in circumstances, and the word *patience* refers to longsuffering with people. Let's personalize this truth.

What challenges are you facing today? Are circumstances overwhelming? Does the bad news keep piling up? Be encouraged. God gives the strength you need to endure difficult circumstances. Are you facing challenges with friends or family members? Are you at odds with coworkers, neighbors, or even people in the church? Be encouraged. God will give the patience you need to endure difficult people.

You are empowered for challenges through Christ.

3. You are empowered for missions through Christ (Col. 1:27,29).

"God wanted to make known among the Gentiles the glorious wealth of this mystery, which is Christ in you, the hope of glory... I labor for this, striving with His strength that works powerfully in me."

In chapter 3, we addressed the mystery of God. While the Old Testament saints anticipated that the Messiah would be among us, no one could have guessed that He would reside within us. His indwelling presence is essential to understanding "His strength that works powerfully in me." As Christ resides in us, His strength also resides in us.

Paul shared about "Christ in you, the hope of glory." However, he did not share this truth in his own strength. According to verse 29, Paul was "striving with His (Christ's) strength that works powerfully in me." Paul learned how to tap into a different source for strength.

Could it be that our evangelistic efforts fall flat because we are striving in our strength? Is it possible that Christians burn out as witnesses for Christ, not because they share too often, but because they've never understood how to tap into Christ's strength within them?

Go back to John 15:4-5. Jesus reveals how we tap into His strength. If a branch is disconnected from the vine, it dries up, becomes brittle, and dies. Our strength is in Christ. Therefore, our job is to abide in the Vine. As we abide in Him, His strength is in us, and He bears fruit through us. Tapping into God's strength is as simple as remaining in close fellowship with Christ.

You and I can be effective witnesses for Christ. As we abide in the Vine, we are empowered for missions through Christ.

WORD STUDY

Labor ... striving

The verb "labor" in 1:29 means to work until it hurts, until muscles are sore and joints ache. Similarly, the verb "strive" referred to the agonizing efforts of an athlete who expends every ounce of his energy in a contest. This imagery expresses that Paul gave his all to the task of proclaiming the truth to God's people so that they would be found pleasing to God when they appeared before Him. However, to avoid the impression that Paul's intense efforts had the ability in and of themselves to grant perfection, Paul closed the paragraph by expressing his complete reliance on divine power. He piled up the references to divine power in such a way that divine power becomes the focus. (CQ)

4. You are empowered for a righteous life through Christ (Col. 3:5–4:6).

Earlier in this chapter, I shared that Colossians easily divides into two sections. The first two chapters address proper belief; the second two chapters call for proper behavior. Our actions are enabled once truth has been established.

In chapter 1, Paul taught believers that they were empowered to bear spiritual fruit through Christ (1:5b-6), empowered for challenges through Christ (1:11), and empowered for missions through Christ (1:27,29). In their own strength, they didn't have the power for any of those things. But then they learned the mystery of God. They discovered that Christ dwells in them. As a result of His life, and His strength in them, they became empowered for a righteousness life. Let's describe what that means.

To be empowered for righteousness is the ability to live righteously. It is the ability to walk in obedience to the commands of God. Apart from Christ, we are slaves to sin. With Christ, we "became enslaved to righteousness" (Rom. 6:18). God enables us to live as He desires.

Have you ever tried to stop doing bad things and start doing good things? The results are mixed at best. We can make small modifications through discipline and determination, but we do not have the power for deep character related changes. I'm convinced that the vast majority of Christians really want to live righteously. They want to be free of lust, greed, jealousy, lying, idolatry, pride, anger, and so forth. However, the desire to be free is not the same as the power to be free.

That's why Paul's teachings on the indwelling Christ are so important. Now that Christ lives in us, we have both the desire and the power to act. "For it is God who is working in you, enabling you both to desire and to work out His good purpose" (Phil. 2:13). God gives both the desire and the enablement to live righteously.

Once we understand that Christ is in us (giving both the desire and power to act), we can embrace the righteous life that Paul described. Colossians 3:5-11 says:

> Therefore, put to death what belongs to your worldly nature: sexual immorality, impurity, lust, evil desire, and greed, which is idolatry. Because of these, God's wrath comes on the disobedient, and you once walked in these things when you were living in them. But now you must also put away all the following: anger, wrath, malice, slander, and filthy language from your mouth. Do not lie to one another, since you have put off

the old self with its practices and have put on the new self. You are being renewed in knowledge according to the image of your Creator. In Christ there is not Greek and Jew, circumcision and uncircumcision, barbarian, Scythian, slave and free; but Christ is all and in all.

Paul tells us to "put to death what belongs to your worldly nature." Remember, in your strength, you do not have the power to put these things to death. However, you have been empowered for righteousness through the indwelling Christ. "You once walked in these things," but "you are being renewed in knowledge according to the image of your Creator." Our ability to live righteously is activated as we are "renewed in the knowledge...of your Creator." Truth precedes enablement.

A CLOSER LOOK

Put to death (3:5)

In Romans 6:11, Paul urged believers to "consider yourselves dead to sin, but alive to God in Christ Jesus." The command in Colossians 3:5 is very similar. Believers should reflect on the significance of their death and resurrection with Christ and should live in light of those realities. (CQ)

WORD STUDY

Sexual immorality is a broad term that includes all sexual sins such as extramarital sex, premarital sex, prostitution, and incest.

Impurity refers to sins that are particularly vile and unnatural. Romans 1:24-27 points to homosexuality and lesbianism as examples of such impurity.

Lust refers to the shameful passions that lead to immoral sexual acts.

Evil desire refers to a craving for forbidden things. In one ancient text, drunkenness, gluttony, and gambling were listed as examples of such evil desires.

Greed refers to the desire to have more than one needs. Paul equated such materialism with **idolatry**, since it is a subtle form of worshiping created things rather than the Creator himself (Eph. 5:5).

Left: A Christian stele from the Coptic Period. The decoration of this stele, in very high relief, shows the figure of a man in Greco-Roman dress, with his hands upraised in an attitude of prayer. He stands in a chapel whose pediment is supported by papyrus columns. Ancient Egyptian temples often were reused as churches after the advent of Christianity in Egypt.

Far left: Ostracon Skeat. A Hymn to Christ on a pottery shard.

Anger refers to an intense displeasure that may flare up in a moment and quickly subside.

Wrath refers to anger that festers and grows until it explodes in a violent expression.

Malice refers to the desire to do harm to others.

Slander refers to words that insult and defame another. "Slander" in the modern sense normally refers to shameful criticisms that are untrue, thus the truthfulness of a criticism is an absolute legal defense against the charge that one has committed slander. However, the Greek term translated "slander" refers to any disrespectful talk. A criticism need not be untrue to constitute slander by a biblical definition.

Filthy language refers to obscene speech. Such talk may be shameful and dirty because it utilizes vocabulary that is profane and crude or because it focuses on shameful topics (Eph. 5:11).

While 3:5-11 challenge us to walk away from unrighteousness, verses 12-17 call us to embrace righteousness. We are to do the following.

- Put on heartfelt compassion, kindness, humility, gentleness, and patience (3:12).
- Accept one another and forgive one another (3:13).
- Put on love (3:14).
- Allow the peace of the Messiah to control your hearts (3:15).
- Be thankful (3:15).
- Let the message about the Messiah dwell richly among you, teaching and admonishing one another in all wisdom, and singing psalms, hymns, and spiritual songs, with gratitude in your hearts to God (3:16).
- Do everything in the name of the Lord Jesus, giving thanks to God the Father through Him (3:17).

WORD STUDY

Heartfelt compassion is a well-known attribute of God (Ex. 34:6; Pss. 25:6; 51:1; 86:15; 103:8; 145:8-9). Such compassion is essential to godliness.

Kindness (the Greek term is sometimes translated "goodness" or "graciousness") is another important divine quality (Ps. 34:8; Luke 6:35). Kindness inspires believers to treat others far better than they deserve, just as God has treated believers far better than they deserve.

Humility is the opposite of the pride which prompts one to boast. Paul probably listed humility among the virtues that believers should pursue because the false teachers promoted a cheap imitation of humility (Col. 2:23) even while they flaunted their supposed superiority by judging others (Col. 2:16) and serving as their spiritual umpires (Col. 2:18). The legalism of the false teachers fostered a judgmental attitude and a haughty spirit. A good dose of Christ-like humility would put a stop to such divisive behavior.

Gentleness is the opposite of "malice," the desire to harm others (Col. 3:8). "Gentleness" (literally "meekness") is the characteristic that prompts believers to bless those that treat them badly. Numbers 12:3 presented Moses as the paragon of gentleness because he prayed for Miriam's healing after God punished her for undermining Moses' authority.

Patience is yet another important characteristic of God (Ex. 34:6). Because of His patience, God is "slow to anger." He grants sinners opportunity to repent before He unleashes His wrath. Such patience is the opposite of the "anger, wrath, and malice" (Col. 3:8) that characterized the Colossians before they became Christians.

That list is a tall order if we are drawing from our own strength. In ourselves, we do not have the ability to walk away from unrighteousness and embrace righteousness. However, the impossible becomes possible through the strength of the indwelling Christ.

The challenge keeps getting bigger. Not only are Christians called to live righteously, but in Colossians 3:18–4:6, we are challenged to submit every aspect of our life to God's control. We learn God's desire for…

- Husbands and wives (3:18-19)
- Children and parents (3:20-21)
- Slaves and owners (3:22-25)
- Rightness and fairness (4:1)
- Prayer, alertness, and thanksgiving (4:2)
- Wisdom with outsiders (4:5)
- Making the most of our time (4:5)
- Gracious speech (4:6)
- A ready answer (4:6)

Are you struggling in your marriage? God gives the desire and enablement to live righteously. Are you unsure of what is right and fair? God will give you the wisdom you need and the power to act upon that wisdom. Do you find yourself wasting time? Allow the indwelling Christ to guide and empower you to make the most of your time. God's commands are accompanied by God's enablement.

Let all of the commands from chapters 3–4 sink in for a moment. Many people are startled to hear that there are 613 commands in the Old Testament. We are quick to praise God for living under grace. Many people are even more startled to hear that there are 1,050 commands in the New Testament. God's desire for righteous living was not diminished at the cross. The difference is that New Testament believers have been given both the desire and the power to live righteously (Phil. 2:13).

You are empowered for a righteousness life through Christ. It may not feel like you are empowered when you're struggling with temptation. I encourage you to believe what God has declared. You are empowered for a righteous life through Christ.

Personal Reflection

1. We are empowered through Christ. In what areas are you trying to do it yourself? What sins are you trying to conquer? What doors are you trying to push through? Where are you working in your strength and not His?

2. If you are empowered through Christ, list several reasons why you feel powerless.

3. When will Jesus be enough? Christians make a lot of excuses for why we need to do things ourselves. Based on everything we've studied, when will Jesus be enough?

CONCLUSION

Christ Is All You Need

We started this study with that statement and we will end the study with the same statement. In the previous 7 chapters, you've seen that...

- You are secure in Christ (Col. 1:15-19).
- You are reconciled in Christ (Col. 1:13-14, 20-22a).
- You are complete in Christ (Col. 1:22, 27-28; 2:2-3,9-10).
- You have a new nature in Christ (Col. 2:11-15; 3:9-10).
- You are free in Christ (Col. 2:16-23).
- You are positioned in Christ (Col. 3:1-4).
- You are empowered through Christ (Col. 1:5b-6,11,27,29; 3:5–4:6).

Christ is all you need.

When you were separated from God because of sin, Christ reconciled you to God. When you were searching for identity, Jesus became your life. When you were hopeless, He gave you hope. When you were dead in sin, He offered His life. There is no challenge that you will face, no obstacle that you will encounter, no pain that you will endure that Christ cannot bring you through.

This conclusion should not be the end; it is only the beginning of a new journey in Christ. You know the truth about the Christ-life. You've seen for yourself that Christianity is not trying harder, but trusting more. God is not asking you to live for Him; He wants to live His life through you.

Our job is to believe what God has said, to abide as branches in the Vine, and to enjoy the fullness of knowing God. Day by day, week by week, and year by year, your life will only confirm Paul's theme.

Christ is all you need.

Two Ways to Earn Credit
for Studying LifeWay Christian Resources Material

CHRISTIAN GROWTH STUDY PLAN

CONTACT INFORMATION:
Christian Growth Study Plan
One LifeWay Plaza, MSN 117
Nashville, TN 37234
CGSP info line 1-800-968-5519
www.lifeway.com/CGSP
To order resources 1-800-485-2772

Christian Growth Study Plan resources are available for course credit for personal growth and church leadership training.

Courses are designed as plans for personal spiritual growth and for training current and future church leaders. To receive credit, complete the book, material, or activity. Respond to the learning activities or attend group sessions, when applicable, and show your work to your pastor, staff member, or church leader. Then go to www.lifeway.com/CGSP, or call the toll-free number for instructions for receiving credit and your certificate of completion.

For information about studies in the Christian Growth Study Plan, refer to the current catalog online at the CGSP Web address. This program and certificate are free LifeWay services to you.

Need a CEU?

CONTACT INFORMATION:
CEU Coordinator
One LifeWay Plaza, MSN 150
Nashville, TN 37234
Info line 1-800-968-5519
www.lifeway.com/CEU

Receive Continuing Education Units (CEUs) when you complete group Bible studies by your favorite LifeWay authors.

Some studies are approved by the Association of Christian Schools International (ACSI) for CEU credits. Do you need to renew your Christian school teaching certificate? Gather a group of teachers or neighbors and complete one of the approved studies. Then go to www.lifeway.com/CEU to submit a request form or to find a list of ACSI-approved LifeWay studies and conferences. Book studies must be completed in a group setting. Online courses approved for ACSI credit are also noted on the course list. The administrative cost of each CEU certificate is only $10 per course.